CONSTITUTIONAL
AMENDMENTS
BEYOND THE BILL OF RIGHTS

P9-CLG-380

Amendment XII
Presidential
Election Process

Other Books of Related Interest

Opposing Viewpoints Series

Civil Liberties

Feminism

Race Relations

Work

Working Women

Current Controversies Series

Civil Liberties

Extremist Groups

Feminism

Human Rights

CONSTITUTIONAL
AMENDMENTS
BEYOND THE BILL OF RIGHTS

Amendment XII
Presidential
Election Process

Jared Zacharias, Book Editor

GREENHAVEN PRESS
A part of Gale, Cengage Learning

GALE
CENGAGE Learning

Detroit • New York • San Francisco • New Haven, Conn • Waterville, Maine • London

GALE
CENGAGE Learning™

Christine Nasso, *Publisher*
Elizabeth Des Chenes, *Managing Editor*

© 2009 Greenhaven Press, a part of Gale, Cengage Learning.

Gale and Greenhaven Press are registered trademarks used herein under license.

For more information, contact:
Greenhaven Press
27500 Drake Rd.
Farmington Hills, MI 48331-3535
Or you can visit our Internet site at gale.cengage.com

ALL RIGHTS RESERVED.
No part of this work covered by the copyright herein may be reproduced, transmitted, stored, or used in any form or by any means graphic, electronic, or mechanical, including but not limited to photocopying, recording, scanning, digitizing, taping, Web distribution, information networks, or information storage and retrieval systems, except as permitted under Section 107 or 108 of the 1976 United States Copyright Act, without the prior written permission of the publisher.

For product information and technology assistance, contact us at

Gale Customer Support, 1-800-877-4253
For permission to use material from this text or product, submit all requests online at www.cengage.com/permissions

Further permissions questions can be emailed to permissionrequest@cengage.com

Articles in Greenhaven Press anthologies are often edited for length to meet page requirements. In addition, original titles of these works are changed to clearly present the main thesis and to explicitly indicate the author's opinion. Every effort is made to ensure that Greenhaven Press accurately reflects the original intent of the authors. Every effort has been made to trace the owners of copyrighted material.

Cover photograph © Najlah Feanny/Corbis.

LIBRARY OF CONGRESS CATALOGING-IN-PUBLICATION DATA

Amendment XII : presidential election process / Jared Zacharias, book editor.
   p. cm. -- (Constitutional amendments: beyond the Bill of Rights)
  Includes bibliographical references and index.
  ISBN 978-0-7377-4123-0 (hardcover)
  1. Election law--United States--History--Juvenile literature. 2. President--United States--Election--Juvenile literature. 3. United States. Constitution. 12th Amendment-- History--Juvenile literature. 4. Electoral college--United States--Juvenile literature. I. Zacharias, Jared. II. Title: Amendmen ttwelve. III. Title: Amendment 12.
  KF4910.A96 2009
  342.73'07--dc22
                                    2008034551

Printed in the United States of America
1 2 3 4 5 6 7 12 11 10 09 08

Contents

Chapter 1: Historical Background on the Twelfth Amendment

The contested election of 1800 magnifies the need for an amendment that would ensure there would be specific ballots for president and vice president and no longer the possibility of a tie between two running mates.

The U.S. House of Representatives, which had to break the tied electoral vote between Thomas Jefferson and Aaron Burr in the election of 1800, debates the need for altering the way electors vote for president and vice president.

The U.S. Senate, responding to the House's proposed constitutional amendment, debates the election issue in its chamber and raises new concerns.

Congress debates the need for amending the Constitution in response to the problems raised with the election of 1800. After being approved by Congress, the amendment goes to the states where further debate ensues.

Chapter 2: Testing the Twelfth Amendment

Presidential Election Process

"Today's Constitution is a realistic document of freedom only because of several corrective amendments. Those amendments speak to a sense of decency and fairness."

Thurgood Marshall

While the U.S. Constitution forms the backbone of American democracy, the amendments make the Constitution a living, ever-evolving document. Interpretation and analysis of the Constitution inform lively debate in every branch of government, as well as among students, scholars, and all other citizens, and views on various articles of the Constitution have changed over the generations. Formally altering the Constitution, however, can happen only through the amendment process. The Greenhaven Press series The Bill of Rights examines the first ten amendments to the Constitution. Constitutional Amendments: Beyond the Bill of Rights continues the exploration, addressing key amendments ratified since 1791.

The process of amending the Constitution is painstaking. While other options are available, the method used for nearly every amendment begins with a congressional bill that must pass both the Senate and the House of Representatives by a two-thirds majority. Then the amendment must be ratified by three-quarters of the states. Many amendments have been proposed since the Bill of Rights was adopted in 1791, but only seventeen have been ratified.

It may be difficult to imagine a United States where women and African Americans are prohibited from voting, where the federal government allows one human being to enslave another, or where some citizens are denied equal protection under the law. While many of our most fundamental liberties are protected by the Bill of Rights, the amendments that followed have significantly broadened and enhanced the rights of American citizens. Such rights may be taken for granted today, but when the amendments were ratified, many were considered groundbreaking and proved to be explosively controversial.

Each volume in Constitutional Amendments provides an in-depth exploration of an amendment and its impact through primary and secondary sources, both historical and contemporary. Primary sources include landmark Supreme Court rulings, speeches by prominent experts, and newspaper editorials. Secondary sources include historical analyses, law journal articles, book excerpts, and magazine articles. Each volume first presents the historical background of the amendment, creating a colorful picture of the circumstances surrounding the amendment's passage: the campaigns to sway public opinion, the congressional debates, and the struggle for ratification. Next, each volume examines the ways the court system has been used to test the validity of the amendment and addresses the ramifications of the amendment's passage. The final chapter of each volume presents viewpoints that explore current controversies and debates relating to ways in which the amendment affects our everyday lives.

Numerous features are included in each Constitutional Amendments volume:

- An originally written introduction presents a concise yet thorough overview of the amendment.

- A time line provides historical context by describing key events, organizations, and people relating to the ratification of the amendment, subsequent court cases, and the impact of the amendment.

- An annotated table of contents offers an at-a-glance summary of each primary and secondary source essay included in the volume.

- The complete text of the amendment, followed by a "plain English" explanation, brings the amendment into clear focus for students and other readers.

- Graphs, charts, tables, and maps enhance the text.

- A list of all twenty-seven Constitutional Amendments offers quick reference.

- An annotated list of court cases relevant to the amendment broadens the reader's understanding of the judiciary's role in interpreting the Constitution.

- A bibliography of books, periodicals, and Web sites aids readers in further research.

- A detailed subject index allows readers to quickly find the information they need.

With the aid of this series, students and other researchers will become better informed of their rights and responsibilities as American citizens. Constitutional Amendments: Beyond the Bill of Rights examines the roots of American democracy, bringing to life the ways the Constitution has evolved and how it has impacted this nation's history.

Amendment Text and Explanation

The Twelfth Amendment to the United States Constitution

Passed by Congress December 9, 1803. Ratified June 15, 1804.

Note: A portion of Article II, Section 1 of the Constitution was superseded by the Twelfth Amendment.

The Electors shall meet in their respective states and vote by ballot for President and Vice-President, one of whom, at least, shall not be an inhabitant of the same state with themselves; they shall name in their ballots the person voted for as President, and in distinct ballots the person voted for as Vice-President, and they shall make distinct lists of all persons voted for as President, and of all persons voted for as Vice-President, and of the number of votes for each, which lists they shall sign and certify, and transmit sealed to the seat of the government of the United States, directed to the President of the Senate;—the President of the Senate shall, in the presence of the Senate and House of Representatives, open all the certificates and the votes shall then be counted;—The person having the greatest number of votes for President, shall be the President, if such number be a majority of the whole number of Electors appointed; and if no person have such majority, then from the persons having the highest numbers not exceeding three on the list of those voted for as President, the House of Representatives shall choose immediately, by ballot, the President. But in choosing the President, the votes shall be taken by states, the representation from each state having one vote; a quorum for this purpose shall consist of a member or members from two-thirds of the states, and a majority of all the states shall be necessary to a choice. [And if the House of Representatives shall not choose a President whenever the right of choice shall devolve upon them, before the fourth day of March next following, then the Vice-President shall act as President, as in case of the death or other constitutional disability of the President.—]* The person having the greatest number of votes as Vice-President, shall be the Vice-President, if such number be a majority of the whole number of Electors appointed, and if no person have a majority, then from the two highest numbers on the list, the Senate shall choose the Vice-President; a quorum for the purpose shall consist of two-thirds of the whole number of Senators, and a majority of the whole number shall be necessary to a choice. But no person constitutionally ineligible to the office of President shall be eligible to that of Vice-President of the United States.

Explanation

Originally, Article II of the U.S. Constitution set up a unique system for electing the president of the United States. Each state was entitled to a number of electoral votes that was determined by how many members of Congress that state was allotted. In order for a candidate to win a presidential election, he needed to win a majority of the electoral votes. Whoever received a majority of the electoral votes became president, and whoever received the second-highest number of votes became the vice president. In the event that there was a tie, the decision was given to the House of Representatives to choose the president and to the Senate to choose the vice president. The Founding Fathers did not foresee the rise of political parties, nor did they desire them. Political parties— the Federalists and the Antifederalists (later Democratic-Republicans)—did, however, appear early on surrounding the debate of national versus regional control. The election of 1800 between Thomas Jefferson, a Democratic-Republican, and John Adams, a Federalist, was a key election. During this election, because of how Article II set up the election of presi-

* Superseded by Section 3 of the Twentieth Amendment.

dents and vice presidents, Jefferson and his running mate, Aaron Burr, tied in the electoral vote. Members of the House of Representatives were thus required to choose the next president, but after thirty-five votes that did not result in a majority, With the thirty-sixth ballot, Thomas Jefferson was finally chosen. Members of Congress and newly elected President Jefferson vowed to fix the system.

The Twelfth Amendment changed the system substantially. It established that each state's electors would cast two ballots—one for the office of president and the other for the office of vice president. The candidate who received a majority of the electoral votes for president would become president, and the candidate who received a majority of the votes for vice president would become vice president. If no candidate obtained a majority of the electoral votes for president, then the House of Representatives would choose from the top three vote-getting presidential candidates. If no candidate obtained a majority of the electoral votes for vice president, then the U.S. Senate would choose from the top two vote-getting vice presidential candidates. The same job requirements that apply to the president also apply to the office of vice president.

The Twelfth Amendment was an attempt to avoid having a system where the Congress would have to continually get involved in presidential elections. The Amendment changed the way the vote was conducted—no longer would electors simply vote for two people; they would have to specify which office each of those candidates was being elected to fill.

Introduction

Long before the Constitutional Convention in 1787, people had discussed ways to select the chief executive of the United States. Thomas Paine, for example, in his renowned essay "Common Sense" (1776), suggested that each colony would send delegates to Congress. One colony would be selected by lottery, and the entire Congress would elect a president from that colony. In the following congressional term, Paine argued that another colony would have its turn of submitting a list of delegates and so on, until all thirteen states had had their chance of having one of their people serve as president. The Continental Congress had been wrestling with the same issue since 1775. At first its members suggested that there should not be one single president; instead, committees should be selected, made up of one delegate from each state.

When the Constitutional Convention met, there was tremendous confusion and lengthy argumentation over the election of the chief executive. Some believed that, because the executive was there simply to carry out the will of the legislature, Congress should appoint the president. Others, citing the method used by certain states according to their state constitutions, argued for presidential election by the people. The initial votes favored the first idea—that a single executive would be chosen by Congress for a term of seven years. Yet the issue was not settled. One member proposed having state governors select a president, but this was rejected. Alexander Hamilton of New York suggested a plan close to what was eventually decided upon: The people in districts already established for the election of senators to Congress would choose individuals called electors, who would in turn elect an executive. The total number of electors would equal the state's representation in Congress. These electors would meet in their own individual states and vote for a president. If anyone obtained a majority of the votes, he would become president. If no one had a majority, a smaller group of electors would vote for one of the three highest candidates.

But as the convention progressed, the issue remained unsettled. Those who wanted the president to be elected by the people continued to argue for that method's value. James Madison of Virginia liked the idea of using electors rather than having an election by the people at large. This time the convention voted in favor of his idea, dropping the plan of having the president selected by the legislature. But that was not the end of the issue. Days later, after more speeches and arguments, the convention reversed its position, saying once again that Congress would elect the president. Madison stressed the value of direct election by the people, but those representing the small states felt that they would have little influence in such an arrangement.

At the end of the convention, the delegates finally settled on the procedure for presidential elections. Each state would appoint a number of electors that would be equal to the total number of senators and representatives the state had in Congress. These electors would meet in their respective states and vote for two people, one of whom could not be an inhabitant of the elector's own state. The person who achieved the majority of electoral votes would become the president, and the person who had the second-highest number of votes would become the vice president. If there was a tie, the House of Representatives would choose from among the top five candidates, with each state being entitled to one vote.

In the first two elections there were no problems with the system. The reason is simple—George Washington was everyone's first choice. From the beginning of the debates over the office of the presidency, everyone knew that Washington would be asked to take on the job. There were no political parties at this time, so it made no difference who was selected as vice president under Washington. John Adams came in second and thus secured the vice presidency.

Problems arose with the election of 1796. By this time political parties had become popular. The Federalists were the party of strong centralized government, whereas the Republicans believed in decentralized power. In 1796 Federalists John Adams and Thomas Pinckney ran against Republicans Thomas Jefferson and Aaron Burr. The election ended up with Adams as president and Jefferson—who received only three fewer votes than Adams—as vice president. This resulted in the president having one set of political beliefs, while his vice president was leader of the opposition.

The nation's fourth election, in 1800, ended in a tie. Jefferson and Burr again challenged President John Adams and his running mate, Charles Cotesworth Pinckney (brother of Thomas Pinckney). On February 11, 1801, Congress tabulated the electoral votes for president and found that Jefferson and Burr had both received seventy-three votes for president (seventy were required for a majority). Republicans hoped that Burr would encourage the election of Jefferson as president, but he never did, leaving many to question his true intentions.

According to the Constitution, the House of Representatives would choose from the top five vote-getters. It began to do so on February 11, 1801, but no candidate was able to get a majority—Jefferson received eight votes, Burr six votes, and two states (Vermont and Maryland) were evenly divided. The days passed, and after thirty-five ballots, the House was still deadlocked. Alexander Hamilton, a prominent Federalist, encouraged his fellow Federalists in the House to vote for Jefferson over Burr because he saw Burr as simply an opportunist. On February 17, after much behind-the-scenes bargaining and political maneuvering, Jefferson gained the vote of ten states.

Shortly after the hotly contested and controversial election of 1800, the House and Senate started to address the issues around electing the president and how to fix the system. In

October 1803 the House passed a resolution that there be separate and specific ballots for the office of president and vice president. This meant that a candidate for president would be elected to that office if he received a majority of the votes for president, and a candidate for vice president would be elected to that office if he received a majority of the votes for vice president. The resolution also reduced from five to three the number of candidates the House would choose from in the event that no one candidate won a majority of the electoral votes.

The Senate, meanwhile, developed a version of the amendment that deviated from the House version largely by requiring that the election of the vice president require a majority of the electors and not just a plurality. On December 2, 1803, the Senate passed its version of the amendment, and on December 8 the House approved it.

Once the amendment was sent to the states for ratification, President Jefferson made it his personal and party's goal to ratify it. He believed that the Federalists were against the amendment purely for partisan reasons—they would be further left out of power because if another Republican was elected to the presidency, his running mate was sure to also be a Republican. By early February 1804 several states had ratified the amendment: North Carolina, Maryland, Kentucky, Ohio, Pennsylvania, Vermont, and Virginia. However, some states did pose problems during the ratification process. Delaware, which had long been a bastion of Federalism, proved to be a longer fight. Republicans in that state had to prove to their fellow statehouse members and the public that, as with Delaware's previous support of the first eleven amendments to the Constitution, it was acceptable to alter the system as long as it was in keeping with the framers' intent. The Republicans were not able to convince the Federalists in the statehouse, and Delaware became the first state to vote against ratification, on January 18, 1804. Only two other loyal Federalist states, Massachusetts and Connecticut, voted with Delaware against the amendment. In late July, Tennessee became the thirteenth state to ratify the amendment, and on September 25, 1804, secretary of state James Madison declared that the Twelfth Amendment had been ratified and would take effect during the upcoming presidential election. It was a tremendous victory for Jefferson and his Republican allies.

The uniqueness of the election system has led to presidential election controversies and anomalies—the winner of the majority of the popular vote has not always become president, and the House has had a role in choosing the president. After ratification of the Twelfth Amendment in 1804, the elections proceeded as expected—parties ran candidates on a ticket, and the winning ticket became the president and vice president. In the election of 1824, the first oddity occurred since the ratification of the Twelfth Amendment. Andrew Jackson, John Quincy Adams, William Harris Crawford, and Henry Clay were all vying for the office of president as members of the Democratic-Republican Party. Each represented a different faction within the party structure, and so it was no surprise that the votes were quite evenly divided among the four men. Because no candidate received the majority of the electoral votes, the House was presented with the top three vote-getters. The House selected John Quincy Adams as the next president despite the fact that Andrew Jackson received more electoral votes than Adams. This election also was the first time that a presidential candidate who received the most popular votes did not become president.

A second odd presidential election took place in 1876. At this point in the nation's history, there were two prominent political parties—the Democrats and Republicans. The Democratic Party selected Samuel J. Tilden as their nominee, and the Republicans chose Rutherford B. Hayes. On the night of the election, it looked like the Democratic nominee would be elected the next president. Tilden had obtained about 3 percent more of the popular vote than Hayes had. However, the states of South Carolina, Louisiana, and Florida were so divided that they delivered two sets of electoral votes to Congress, which then had to establish a special commission to resolve the problem. The congressional commission—after what some considered to be political manipulations—ended up accepting the electoral votes for the Republican, Hayes, from all three disputed states.

The presidential election of 2000 demonstrated an inherent oddity of the electoral college system. The system can allow a candidate to win the popular vote nationwide and still lose the election for president. After all the votes were counted, Democratic candidate Al Gore had received about 540,000 more popular votes than George W. Bush. However, Bush's narrow victory in Florida enabled him to take all of Florida's 25 electoral votes, which secured him 271 votes in the electoral college, compared with Gore's 266 votes. Bush thus became a minority-elected president.

Many voices have called for changing how the United States elects its president. Most of the attacks are leveled squarely at the electoral college system. There have been about seven hundred failed attempts in Congress to change how the electoral college operates. The opponents of the electoral college tend to cite several important reasons for wanting to alter the system. First, advocates of change argue that the current system allows for the election of a president who failed to achieve a majority or even a plurality of the popular vote. This was seen with the elections of 1824, 1876, and 2000. Anti–electoral college advocates argue that such a system ignores the wishes of the people. Second, it is argued that the electoral college might suppress voter turnout. People may feel that their votes do not really matter, since someone else (an elector) is casting the real ballots. Third, some opponents say that the electoral college does not reflect the will of the people, because people in rural states are overrepresented. Lastly, some object to the winner-take-all method that most states use to apportion electoral votes—that is, if Candidate A wins 51 percent of a state's popular vote and Candidate B wins 49 percent of the state's popular vote, Candidate A gets 100 percent of the electoral votes for that state and Candidate B gets none.

Proponents of the electoral college cite the fact that the system encourages regional influence to be spread over a wide area. Rather than allowing a few populous states to pick the president through their overwhelming population numbers, the candidates have to campaign and spend time appealing to smaller states. The electoral college is considered to be a way to ensure that a candidate has to appeal to as many different regions as possible in order to shore up his or her electoral majority vote. Also, the electoral college is seen as ensuring the federal nature of the American political system. The House was created to represent the states based on their population, the Senate to represent the states equally, and the presidency to represent all of the states. Those favoring the electoral college believe that, if the country switched to a popular vote system, the system would devolve into a purely nationalized central government.

The framers of the U.S. Constitution had to be very careful when putting together this new system of government. In establishing the presidency, they had little to no historical information to draw on. Because they based so much of the presidency around the figure of George Washington, they did not realize the potential problems that were created for the election process. These problems quickly required addressing via the Twelfth Amendment. While it is a little-known amendment, it has had a profound effect on the presidency and the nation's history.

Chronology

1787

The U.S. Constitution is crafted and provides for the president to be elected indirectly by the electoral college; electors are appointed by states, which are free to decide how they wish to select their electors. The Constitution provides for the second-place finisher to become vice president. If none of the candidates gains a majority of the votes, the election of the president is sent to the House of Representatives to decide.

1787–1788

Debate ensues between those in favor of ratifying the Constitution (Federalists) and those who are against it and want more local control (Antifederalists). The Federalists believe the squabbles and lack of unity among the states under the Articles of Confederation are proof that a stronger and more centralized government is needed. The Antifederalists believe that the Articles of Confederation could be amended to fix some of the issues. They also believe that a strong, centralized government is not necessary or desired because the country had just cast off a strong centralized government in the form of Great Britain.

1788

The U.S. Constitution is ratified.

1789

The U.S. Constitution formally takes effect, and the first session of Congress is convened. George Washington becomes the first president.

1796

A presidential election occurs between former vice president John Adams, a Federalist, and Thomas Jefferson, someone who strongly opposes the Federalist Party and movement and eventually helps form the Democratic-Republicans. Jefferson loses the election to Adams.

1800

The presidential election again pits John Adams, the incumbent president, against Thomas Jefferson, his vice president.

1800–1801

Thomas Jefferson and Aaron Burr, both from the same party, each receive the same number of electoral votes. Following the constitutionally prescribed rules under Article II, the House of Representatives decides who the next president will be. After thirty-six ballots, the members of the House pick Jefferson instead of Burr. This ordeal leaves members of Congress and President Jefferson with the belief that the Constitution needs to be amended.

1804

The Twelfth Amendment is ratified. It provides for a separate election of the vice president, to avoid the problems associated with the election of 1800.

1824

John Quincy Adams receives fewer electoral and popular votes than Andrew Jackson. However, neither candidate receives a majority of the electoral votes, so the election goes to the U.S. House of Representatives, which selects Adams.

1830s

States gradually move to popular election for their presidential electors.

1876

Rutherford B. Hayes faces Samuel J. Tilden in a disputed presidential election involving confusing votes from three Southern states.

1877

Congress creates an Electoral Commission to resolve the dispute. It splits along party lines to award Hayes the presidency.

1887

The Electoral Vote Count Act specifies that the state legislatures have the authority to adopt their own procedures for selecting their electors.

1892

The U.S. Supreme Court upholds a Michigan law that awards electoral votes by congressional district.

1992

The electoral college fails to give third-party candidate H. Ross Perot any electoral votes even though he wins nearly 20 percent of the national popular vote.

2000

George W. Bush loses the national popular vote to Al Gore but wins the presidency because of the electoral college outcome, which was dependent on the close race in Florida.

CONSTITUTIONAL
AMENDMENTS
BEYOND THE BILL OF RIGHTS

CHAPTER 1

Historical Background on the Twelfth Amendment

The Election of 1800 Exposes a Constitutional Flaw

Doris Faber and Harold Faber

Doris Faber and Harold Faber have written several biographies, including those of Eleanor Roosevelt, American heroes of the twentieth century, and mothers of American presidents. In addition they have written books on law and U.S. history. They both have worked as reporters for the New York Times. *In the following article, the authors present the problems with the electoral college as it was originally defined in the Constitution. They focus on the third presidential election, in 1800, which involved a bitter political rivalry between Thomas Jefferson and the incumbent president, John Adams, leading to a surprising outcome that created a political uproar.*

The ambitions of four prominent men—John Adams, Thomas Jefferson, Alexander Hamilton, and Aaron Burr—clashed during the presidential election of 1800, one of the most complicated ever held throughout American history. While three were candidates—Adams, Jefferson, and Burr—Hamilton was not. Behind the scenes, though, Hamilton exercised the wiles of an astute politician, attempting to maintain his own power as a President-maker.

It was a most unusual election year. For the first and only time in American history, an incumbent President—Adams—was running against an incumbent Vice President—Jefferson. It was also the first election in which clearly recognized political parties competed. The Federalists, with Adams as their standard-bearer, opposed the Democratic-Republicans led by Jefferson.

Doris Faber and Harold Faber, *We the People—The Story of the United States Constitution Since 1787.* New York: Charles Scribner's Sons, 1987. Copyright © 1987 by Doris and Harold Faber. Reproduced by permission.

The result was a stunning surprise that would bring about the adoption of a new amendment to the Constitution. The tally of ballots cast by the official presidential electors produced a tie vote—not between Adams and Jefferson, the opposing candidates seeking the nation's top office, but between Jefferson and Burr, who were running on the same ticket. Even Burr himself had expected to be considered only as Jefferson's Vice President. . . .

In those days before presidential primaries or nominating conventions, candidates were chosen at meetings of members of Congress belonging to each of the parties. Among the Democratic-Republicans, there was no question about who should head their ticket—the current Vice President, Thomas Jefferson. Burr, with the important New York vote under his control, convinced his party's caucus to name him as Jefferson's successor in the vice presidency.

But the Federalists, despite their hold on the White House, were split.

How the Problem Arose

The incumbent President Adams, though a Federalist, had taken some independent positions that defied other leaders of his party—especially on the urgent issue of war or peace with France. Led by Hamilton, most of the Federalists were strongly on the side of the English and against the French in the continuing war between these two countries. They even wanted the United States to help the English defeat France. But Adams had sought to keep the nation out of the conflict by a series of negotiations, which infuriated the more aggressive members of his party.

And so, when the time came for the Federalists to select their candidate for President in 1800, there was bitter opposition to Adams. Still, he had enough supporters to win the nomination. Hamilton, though, could not accept this majority decision, and instead backed the Federalist vice presidential candidate, Charles Cotesworth Pinckney, of South Carolina. Hamilton hoped Pinckney would be able to win most of the electoral votes in the South and enough in the North to give him a chance of winning the presidency, rather than just the lesser post for which he had been named.

In effect, Hamilton was trapped by his antagonism toward both Jefferson and Adams. Hamilton realized that should Pinckney fail, as was most likely, his own refusal to support Adams would give Jefferson the victory. But Hamilton decided he would rather have even Jefferson than a second term for Adams. "If we must have an enemy at the head of the government," he said, "let it be one whom we can oppose, and for whom we are not responsible . . . who will not involve our party in the disgrace of his foolish and bad measures."

None of the candidates that year campaigned for office in the style we know today. As was the custom then, they stayed at home receiving visitors and writing letters. All the campaigning was done by their supporters, who held meetings and filled the newspapers with all sorts of angry attacks. It turned out to be one of the bitterest struggles in American political history.

The Federalists charged that Jefferson had cheated people to whom he owed money, obtained property by fraud, robbed a widow of her estate, and acted cowardly during the Revolutionary War when he was governor of Virginia. They also labeled him an atheist. The Democratic-Republican claims concerning Adams were equally absurd. They called him a hypocrite, a criminal, a tyrant—they even spread the story that he planned to have one of his sons marry one of King George III's daughters, thus starting an American monarchy. . . .

To the framers of the Constitution, a presidential election was a very important matter. They had erected a complex system whereby each state would select electors equal to the combined number of their Senators and Representatives in

Congress. In most states, the electors were chosen by the state legislatures, but in a few they were elected by the people. Each elector had two votes. When the electoral votes of all the states were counted, the person with the highest number of votes would become President and the one with the second highest Vice President.

That system had worked well in 1789 and 1792, when Washington had been elected unanimously, with Adams becoming Vice President. In 1796, the first contested presidential election, the results had been close but clear—Adams received seventy-one electoral votes, Jefferson sixty-eight, Thomas Pinckney of South Carolina fifty-nine, and Burr thirty. Adams became President and Jefferson Vice President, even though they represented opposing political parties.

By then, though, it was obvious that the framers of the Constitution had not foreseen the rise of political parties and had underestimated the intensity of partisan feelings. They had intended the electors to use their independent judgment in electing the President. But it was already apparent that electors considered themselves bound to vote for the candidate of the political party they represented. . . .

The Votes Are Counted

By mail and by courier on horseback, the election returns finally began to reach Washington in December. Toward the end of the month, an unofficial tally disclosed a most upsetting state of affairs: Jefferson had seventy-three electoral votes, Burr also had seventy-three, Adams sixty-five, Pinckney sixty-one, and John Jay one.

The men who wrote the Constitution had foreseen possible problems. They had provided that, if any candidate did not have a majority, it would be up to the House of Representatives to choose the winner. . . .

On February 11, 1801, in an atmosphere of tension, while a snowstorm raged outside, a joint session of Congress met to count the electoral votes officially. As provided for in the Constitution, the Vice President—Jefferson—sat in the chair of the president of the Senate while the votes to decide his own future were counted. The outcome was precisely as expected: a tie vote, with seventy-three for both Jefferson and Burr.

The U.S. House Must Decide

As a result, the election was thrown into the House of Representatives where, under the rules set by the Constitution, a majority vote of nine of the sixteen states, with each state voting as a unit, was necessary to decide the winner. The first tally proved indecisive. Jefferson got eight states—New York, New Jersey, Pennsylvania, Virginia, North Carolina, Kentucky, Georgia, and Tennessee. Six states—New Hampshire, Massachusetts, Rhode Island, Connecticut, Delaware, and South Carolina—cast their ballots for Burr. Two states—Maryland and Vermont—were tied within their own delegations and so voted for neither candidate.

In the cold, unheated chamber of the House, its members continued to vote, time after time. From one o'clock in the afternoon, all through the night until eight o'clock the next morning, twenty-seven separate ballots were taken. All had the same results, eight states for Jefferson, six for Burr, two blank. Not one delegate or one state had changed. After the thirty-third ballot, the weary legislators decided to adjourn over the weekend.

That weekend, there were several private meetings. It was reported that some Federalists approached Burr and attempted to make a deal with him. But, as one wrote later, Burr rejected any deal and lost his chance to become President. Other Federalists sent an intermediary to meet with Jefferson and try to reach an understanding with him. Jefferson later denied that any bargain was made.

But when the House reconvened after the weekend, a few Federalist votes changed. In Maryland and Vermont, some

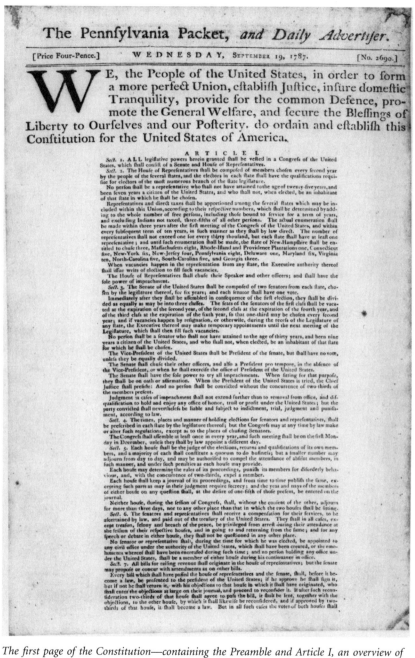

The first page of the Constitution—containing the Preamble and Article I, an overview of the Legislative Branch—was published on the cover of the Pennsylvania Packet two days after the Constitution was signed. The Library of Congress.

congressmen who had voted for Burr now cast blank ballots, with the result that their states went for Jefferson. On the thirty-sixth ballot, Jefferson had ten states, one more than the nine required, and was declared the next President.

The transition of power from one political party to the other, the first such transfer in the United States, went peacefully but with extreme bitterness. The Federalists, who still controlled Congress, hastily passed two judiciary acts creating many new judges in the federal courts and justices of the peace in the District of Columbia. In his famous "midnight appointments," Adams filled the vacancies with faithful Federalists. . . .

Jefferson tried in his inaugural address to smooth over the partisan bitterness. "We are all Republicans, we are all Federalists," he said, calling for unity in the years ahead.

At least on one matter, almost everyone agreed. It was that a constitutional change was needed to prevent a recurrence of the recent disputed election. Other pressing problems intervened, though, and not till 1803 did Congress propose the Twelfth Amendment.

The House of Representatives Tackles the Problem of Presidential Elections

U.S. House of Representatives

The following viewpoint highlights the actual debate in the House of Representatives surrounding whether to adopt an amendment to the Constitution to change how elections for president and vice president are handled. Members discuss changing the amendment's wording, the role of the House in close presidential elections, the possibility of direct election of the president, and the possible influence of the large states.

The House resolved itself into a Committee of the Whole on the report of a select committee on propositions of amendment to the Constitution.

The report was read, as follows:

Resolved, by the Senate and House of Representatives of the United States of America in Congress assembled, two-thirds of both Houses concurring, That the following article be proposed to the Legislatures of the different States as an amendment to the Constitution of the United States, which, when ratified by three-fourths of the said Legislatures, shall be valid to intents and purposes as a part of the said Constitution, viz:

"In all future elections of President and Vice President, the Electors shall name in their ballots the person voted for as President, and in distinct ballots the person voted for as Vice President, of whom one at least shall not be an inhabitant of the same State with themselves. The person having a

U.S. House of Representatives, "Amendment to the Constitution, 8th Congress, 1st Session," in *History of Congress*, pp. 420–430. http://memory.loc.gov/cgi-bin/ampage?collId=llac&fileName=013/llac013.db&recNum=182.

majority of all the Electors for President shall be the President; and if there shall be no such majority, the President shall be chosen from the highest numbers, not exceeding three, on the list for President, by the House of Representatives, in the manner directed by the Constitution. The person having the greatest number of votes as Vice President shall be the Vice President, and in case of an equal number of votes for two or more persons for Vice President, they being the highest on the list, the Senate shall choose the Vice President from those having such equal number, in the manner directed by the Constitution."

Mr. [John] Dawson observed, that at the time of the adoption of the Constitution, that part of it which related to the election of a President and Vice President had been objected to; and evils likely to occur had been foreseen by some gentlemen at that day. Experience had shown that they were not mistaken. Every gentleman in that House knew the situation in which the country had been placed by the controverted election of a Chief Magistrate; it was one which he trusted never would return. . . .

Alteration of the Amendment

Mr. J. Clay, though in favor of the principle of the amendment, was of opinion that, as to some of its parts, it required alteration. He therefore moved

"But if no person have such majority, then the House of Representatives shall immediately proceed to choose by ballot from the two persons having the greatest number of votes, one of them for President; or if there be three or more persons having an equal number of votes, then the House of Representatives shall in like manner, from the persons having such equality of votes, choose the President; or if there be one person having a greater number of votes—not being a majority of the whole number of Electors appointed—than any other person, and two or more persons who have an equal number of votes one with the other, then the House of Representatives shall in like manner, from among such persons having the greater number of votes and such other persons having an equality of votes, choose the President."

Mr. [Philip] Van Cortlandt thought the amendment liable to objection.

Mr. G.W. Campbell was in favor of the principle contained in the amendment. He considered to be the duty of this House, in introducing an amendment to the Constitution on this point, to secure to the people the benefits of choosing the President, so as to prevent a contravention of their will as expressed by Electors chosen by them; resorting to Legislative interposition only in extraordinary cases: and when this should be rendered necessary; so guarding the exercise of Legislative power, that those only should be capable of Legislative election who possessed a strong evidence of enjoying the confidence of the people. This was the true spirit and principle of the Constitution, whose object was, through the several organs of the Government, faithfully to express the public opinion. For this reason he was in favor of the proposed amendment. . . .

Mr. J. Clay begged leave explicitly to state, for the satisfaction of the gentleman from Connecticut, that it was not his intention to change that part of the Constitution which prescribed that the votes should be by States; and if it would induce the gentleman to vote for the resolution he had moved, he would add the words of the Constitution, viz:

"But in choosing the President the votes shall be taken by States, the representation from each State having one vote; a quorum for this purpose shall consist of a member or members from two-thirds of the States, and a majority of all the States shall be necessary to a choice."

These words were accordingly added.

Debate on Numbers

Mr. Dawson observed that this proposition had been submitted to the select committee, who had considered it more objectionable than that reported. Their object was to innovate as little as possible on the Constitution. A great part of it referred to cases so extremely remote as were not likely to happen. The only material change it made was to reduce the number of persons from whom a choice should be made from three to two. At present the election for a President and Vice President was made from the five highest on the list. As, according to the proposed amendment, a designation of the persons voted for as President and Vice President was to be made, it was considered that by giving the three highest to the House of Representatives, from which to choose a President, and the two highest to the Senate, from which to choose a Vice President, the spirit of the Constitution would not be changed. He hoped therefore the report of the committee would be agreed to. . . .

Principle of Direct Election

Mr. [John] Clopton said he rose to express his approbation of the amendment offered by the gentleman from Pennsylvania (Mr. Clay.) He said that indeed the amendment could not but be acceptable to him, inasmuch as it corresponded with the ideas he had the honor to express to the Committee on this subject the other day. He begged leave now to make a few remarks in addition to those which he had then stated. He said, if anything is to be lamented as a defect in the fundamental principles of our Government, that defect perhaps consists in a departure from the plain and simple modes of immediate election by the people as to some of the branches of the Government. He did not mean however now to discuss, nor did he know that he ever should discuss, this point. The Constitution of the United States having established a different principle in respect to the election of the several departments of the Government, except that branch of the Legislature which this House composes; and the object of the proposed amendment to the Constitution not being the transmutation of a fundamental principle, but merely an alteration in the mode heretofore directed of electing one branch of the Government according to the principle already established, his business and his object was to state to this Committee those ideas which occurred to him on this occasion as suited to the subject as it now stands before the Committee.

When the framers of this Constitution, said Mr. C., submitted it to the consideration of the people of the several States, drawn as it is, directing the election of President and Vice President to be made through the medium of Electors chosen by the people for that purpose, never could it have been their intention in submitting, or the intention of the people in accepting the Constitution, to admit a principle that any eventual Legislative election would be proper, if the object of it did not bear the stamp of public confidence. They never could have abandoned that great political consideration that the people, as the primary source of all power, should first give to those particular citizens, among whom such Legislative choice might be made, the evidence of a very considerable share of their confidence. The Electors are the organs, who, acting from a certain and unquestioned knowledge of the choice of the people, by whom they themselves were appointed, and under immediate responsibility to them, select and announce those particular citizens, and affix to them by their votes an evidence of the degree of public confidence which is bestowed upon them. The adoption of this medium, through which the election should be made, in preference to the mode of immediate election by the people, was no abandonment of the great principle, that the appointment of the constituted authorities ought to be conformable to the public will. . . .

Mr. [Andrew] Gregg.—It was impossible fully to comprehend the two propositions offered, barely by hearing them read. Amendments to the Constitution were of great importance. He felt at a loss how to act in the present instance, not clearly understanding the resolutions proposed. He was in favor of the principle they contained, and had always been so. He had been in Congress in the year 1796 when the first proposition to this effect was made by a gentleman from New Hampshire.

Keep It Simple

The inconveniences attending the last election had strengthened his conviction of the propriety of an amendment similar in substance to that offered. He viewed, therefore, with pleasure the attention now paid to the subject by the House, and hoped an amendment would take place at the present time. The more simple that amendment was, the more likely it would be to be approved by the States. In order ultimately to simplify it, so as to render it the least objectionable to the States, he wished every member, who had formed in his mind an eligible proposition, would now bring it forward, that the whole might be printed.

Mr. J. Clay said, as there existed considerable difference of opinion, he would withdraw his motion in order to move that the Committee should rise, when he would move a recommitment of the report of the select committee.

Mr. [Joseph] Nicholson said that before the question was taken on the rising of the Committee, he would offer an amendment to the resolution reported by the select committee. It was his opinion that the question of principle should be settled in the House; if not so settled, it would be impossible for the report of any select committee to meet the approbation of the House. In the select committee a variety of propositions had been offered; the Committee reported one, to which they had agreed; there were still endless amendments offered, which he was convinced would continue to be offered until some principle was fixed by the House. In making an amendment to the Constitution on this point, they ought to guard against all possible difficulties. The amendment of the gentleman from Pennsylvania goes to guard against those difficulties. But cases may arise in which the amendment of the select committee will not be adequate. . . .

Trust in Electors and the House

Mr. [Calvin] Goddard said, though he would not pledge himself to vote for the proposed amendment to the Constitution, in any shape whatever, yet he was in favor of the amendment offered by the gentleman from Maryland. He thought with him that there would be no great danger from the latitude allowed the House of Representatives, as they were chosen by the people as well as the Electors; nor could he perceive why they were more to be distrusted than the Electors. But the principal reason that operated with him in favor of the amendment was that it extended the right of suffrage in the House of Representatives. It is well known that our system is that of a Confederation. There appeared to him no danger of 176 persons being voted for; the nature of the Government was such that but few persons would be voted for. But, if no choice is made by the Electors, he wished the right of the House of Representatives to be extended for this reason, because it will increase the power of the small States. As he conceived, the original proposition went effactually to impair the rights of the small States; and indeed, any amendment would have that effect; but the amendment of the gentleman from Maryland having this effect as little as possible: he should vote for it. . . .

Mr. [Thomas] Sanford said the great object of the amendment ought to be to prevent persons voted for as Vice President from becoming President. If the amendment effected this, it was sufficient. All other innovation upon the Constitution was improper; and no danger could arise from extending the right of the House of Representatives to making a choice from the five highest. . . .

Giving Too Much Power to the House?

Mr. [James] Elliot hoped the amendment of the gentleman from Maryland would not prevail; and coming, as he did himself, from a small State, he trusted the House would pardon him for assigning his reasons for that hope. He felt as much confidence in the House of Representatives as the gentleman from Connecticut; but he was of opinion that their discretion ought to be limited. The amendment will give the House of Representatives the unqualified power of electing from the whole number on the list of persons voted for as President, and on that ground he opposed it. It was said to be a question of larger and smaller States, and those who represent the smaller States were called upon to check the usurpation of the larger States. Our system was undoubtedly federative, and there might be danger of an usurpation of the large States if the small ones were not protected by the Constitution. His wish was that they might be so guarded. But he still thought the discretion of the House of Representatives ought to be limited. . . .

Mr. C. was in favor of preserving that part of the Constitution which directed the election to be made by States, wishing as little innovation as possible on the principles of the Constitution. He did not, however, conceive a mere change of words dangerous, but the establishment of a principle that deprived the people of the power of electing those who possessed the largest share of their confidence. He was decidedly in favor of whatever had this effect, as according with the true spirit of the Constitution; and he was, therefore, opposed to the amendment of the gentleman from Maryland. His own opinion, too, was that it was best to express in one article whatever related to the election of President and Vice President, than refer to the Constitution; by which the provisions on that subject would be rendered much clearer.

Influence of Large States

Mr. [Willis] Alston was opposed to the amendment offered by the gentleman from Pennsylvania (Mr. Smilie) to the amendment of the select committee, because in his opinion it would have a tendency to bring the election of a President of the United States more frequently into the House of Representatives, than otherwise it would be brought; he was as much disposed to guard against the influence of the large States as any member upon that floor.

The gentleman from Connecticut last up (Mr. Goddard) was in favor of the amendment, because he thought it calculated to lessen the influence of larger States. For his part, Mr. A. thought very differently from that gentleman; he believed that, provided the amendment should be acceded to, it would be an inducement to any one of the large States to prevent an election of President by the Electors of the several States, that if the votes of a large State should be withheld from any of the candidates proposed as President, it would prevent such candidate from obtaining a majority of all the votes of the Electors. What then, Mr. A. asked, would be the consequence? The choice would have to be made by that House, which circumstance he never wished to witness again; this he conceived to be an important point to guard against as much as possible.

The Senate Responds to the House's Proposed Amendment

U.S. Senate

The U.S. Senate responded to the House's initiation of an amendment to the Constitution that would change the process for electing the president and vice president by debating a similar proposition. Several members felt that there was a need to delay debate and that this proposed amendment was not necessary nor needed quickly. Still, other members used this debate as an opportunity to discuss the possibility of even eliminating the office of vice president altogether.

Mr. Dayton moved to strike out all which respected the appointment of a Vice President.

He said the great inducements of the framers of the Constitution to admit the office of Vice President was, that, by the mode of choice, the best and most respectable man should be designated; and that the Electors of each State should vote for one person at least, living in a different State from themselves; and if the substance of the amendment was adopted, he thought the office had better be abolished. Jealousies were natural between President and Vice President; no heir apparent ever loved the person on the throne. With this resolution for an amendment to the Constitution we were left with all the inconveniencies, without a single advantage from the office of Vice President.

Mr. Clinton.—The obvious intention of the amendment proposed by the gentleman from New Jersey, is to put off or get rid of the main question. It would more comport with the candor of the gentleman to meet the question fairly. Can the

U.S. Senate, "Amendment to the Constitution, 8th Congress, 1st Session," in *History of Congress*, October 1803, pp. 21–25. http://memory.loc.gov/cgi-bin/ampage?collId=llac &fileName=013//llac013.db&recNum=2.

gentleman suppose that the Electors will not vote for a man of respectability for Vice President? True, the qualifications are distinct, and ought not to be confounded; this will stave off the question till the Legislatures of the States of Tennessee and Vermont are out of session, and the object must be very obvious.

Mr. Dayton— . . .

The reasons of erecting the office are frustrated by the amendment to the Constitution now proposed; it will be preferable, therefore, to abolish the office. . . .

Mr. Nicholas.—To secure the United States from the dangers which existed during the last choice of President, the present resolution was introduced. It was impossible to act upon, or pass the amendment offered by the member from New Jersey, with a full view of all its bearings at this time. It ought not to stand in the way of the resolution reported by the committee, for two-thirds or three-quarters of the State Legislatures would be in session in two or three months; the Senate had, therefore, better not admit the amendment, even if convinced that it was correct, because it might jeopardize the main amendment of discriminating.

Attempt to Postpone Debate

Mr. Butler moved a postponement until Wednesday, because the amendment was important, and he had not had sufficient time to make up his mind.

Mr. Worthington said the same.

This motion was seconded.

Mr. Cocke was opposed to the postponement, because he feared the State Legislatures would be out of session, so as not to carry the amendment into effect before the next choice of President. . . .

Mr. Jackson did not know how he should vote on the amendment offered by the gentleman from New Jersey, but was willing to indulge the gentleman who asked for a postponement. What were the ideas of gentlemen? Were the State Legislatures all about to die? If they were not in session when Congress had acted upon this amendment they could be called together. He remembered that the Vice President was called the fifth wheel to a coach, many years ago, and it might be well, now we are on the subject, to examine whether the office cannot be dispensed with. We have time enough.

Mr. Hillhouse.—So important was this subject, that he wished for more time; the gentleman from New York thinks the two offices are very diverse; (here he cited the Constitution, by which the duties of the President devolve on the Vice President in certain cases;) he thought it worthy of mature consideration, if the discriminating principle was introduced into the choice of Vice President, whether the office had not better be abolished. . . .

Mr. S. Smith mentioned that the last choice of President had prepared the people to require the discrimination; but the abolition of the office was new. If the choice of Vice President in the way proposed, should, upon experiment, prove to be improper, then it could be altered. . . .

The question for postponement was taken, and lost—ayes 15, noes 16.

A New Direction for the Debate

The amendment of Mr. Dayton was now before the Senate.

Mr. Adams thought the discriminating principle was well understood; but the consequences had not been fully contemplated; one was, the abolition of the office of Vice President. Whether it was best to abolish or not, he would not say, but to consider it with the other subject was certainly correct, and he wished for longer time.

Mr. Maclay could not see that any new principle was introduced by the committee; he thought that a suggestion that an improper person would be chosen Vice President was premature; it could not be known till tried.

Aaron Burr became vice president of the United States after tying with Thomas Jefferson at 73 votes each in the Electoral College. Burr served in that position from 1801 to 1805. The Library of Congress.

Mr. Breckinridge said his mind was made up to vote for nothing but the discriminating principle, so his constituents wished; and he would not go into consideration of any other amendments, but wished this to go into operation before the

45

next election. His opinion was, that the duration of the office in the Senate, (six years,) was the most anti-republican he could conceive of, but if he moved that and connected it with the discriminating principle, he might lose all; he was against a postponement.

Mr. White was convinced that the members were unprepared to act, and particularly so, by what fell from the member last up, and moved a postponement until to-morrow.

This motion was seconded by Mr. Butler. . . .

Mr. Butler was alarmed at what he saw this day; he wished to take a long and deep view of this subject, and there was not time now, the day was far spent; he rather thought the office of Vice President might be abolished, but he would not commit himself now; he wished for time, not to discredit, by a hasty decision, the States from which the Senate came. . . .

Mr. Dayton said that he had already stated to the Senate that he conceived himself impelled by a sense of duty to offer the amendment under consideration for abolishing altogether the office of Vice President, if the change which was proposed to be made in the mode of electing the President should prevail. When gentlemen had considered the subject too important to be decided upon that day, he felt disposed to indulge them with a reasonable time for consideration, and he hoped that the postponement they asked for would be consented to. . . .

A motion for adjournment was now made and carried—ayes 16, noes 15.

The Course of the Debate from Congress to Ratification

Lolabel House

This viewpoint was written in 1901 by Lolabel House for her PhD dissertation. The author discusses how Congress debated the need for changing the election system for the presidency. However, after it was approved by Congress, the amendment still had to be sent to the states for ratification. The states conducted further argument surrounding the proposed Twelfth Amendment.

One of the most interesting things noted in going over the debates is the completeness with which the parties change sides on the question of State Rights. One Federalist made the declaration that the Resolution, by impairing the rights of the small States in choosing the President, destroyed the basis of the Confederacy, and made the Constitution a *nudum pactum* [a "naked contract," unenforceable]. The most extreme grounds on both sides, however, were taken by the Republican, Campbell (Va.) and the Federalist, Dennis (Md.).

The Issue of State Rights

Campbell argued for government by simple majorities and anticipated the arguments of Webster on his memorable debate with Hayne. Starting with the words, "We, the people of the United States," he argued that the government was formed by the people of the United States in their capacity as such, by their immediate representatives in the general convention and not by the several States convened in their State capacities. This statement had about as much historical foundation as did the statement of Webster in 1830, that "this government is

Lolabel House, "A Study of the Twelfth Amendment of the Constitution of the United States," in *A Study of the Twelfth Amendment of the Constitution of the United States*, University of Pennsylvania, Philadelphia, 1901, pp. 55–61.

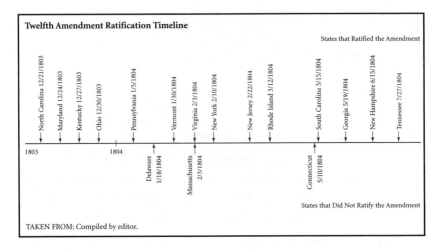

Twelfth Amendment Ratification Timeline

States that Ratified the Amendment

North Carolina 12/21/1803
Maryland 12/24/1803
Kentucky 12/27/1803
Ohio 12/30/1803
Pennsylvania 1/5/1804
Vermont 1/30/1804
Virginia 2/3/1804
New York 2/10/1804
New Jersey 2/22/1804
Rhode Island 3/12/1804
South Carolina 5/15/1804
Georgia 5/19/1804
New Hampshire 6/15/1804
Tennessee 7/27/1804

1803
1804

Delaware 1/18/1804
Massachusetts 2/3/1804
Connecticut 5/10/1804

States that Did Not Ratify the Amendment

TAKEN FROM: Compiled by editor.

the independent offspring of the popular will." To this doctrine Dennis replied that in a single State a simple majority ought to prevail, but he denied that to be the theory at the basis of the Union. He declared that the Constitution was not adopted by the people of the United States, but by the people of the several States, as such, voting through the medium of their State Conventions, and so far from having been adopted by the people of the United States, as such, it was doubtful whether it was not adopted by a minority of the people, though ratified by a majority of the States.

Constitutional Versus Popular Majorities

Campbell entirely overlooked the Constitution as the supreme of the land and advocated the doctrine that "the will of the people should be supreme." He confounded constitutional with popular majorities. The American principle is that the former shall rule and in many cases they do not at all coincide with the latter. These constitutional majorities differ in different cases. The most striking example of this is in the representation in the Senate, and to a less degree in the House, due to the fact that each State must have at least one representative. Another illustration is in the change from a simple majority to a two-third vote necessary to pass a bill over a veto or to pass an amendment. Apart from the federative principle, this rule of constitutional majorities must be preserved for the protection of the minority. It is an essential principle in the political life of the United States that there be preserved to the minority the negative power of acting as a brake; the conservative power by which it keeps itself from being crushed.

The Independence of the Electors

Another question involved in the amendment was that of the independence of the electors. The intention of the Convention had been that men of ability and discretion should be chosen for this duty and that they should exercise this discretion in the choice of President. By 1800 they had begun to feel the pressure of party choice as almost irresistible, but the amendment, by making party government constitutional and imperative, completed the process of making them "men of straw." Since its adoption they have been, as a usual thing, men upon whom it was desired to confer some honor, but beyond that they might as well be automata [robots]. The desire expressed by [John] Breckinridge during the debates that the choice of President should be made directly by the people has been realized to an extent that would have gratified James Wilson and Gouverneur Morris, but would have caused other prominent members of the Convention of 1787 to be alarmed at what they denominated the "Monster of Democracy."

Jefferson expressed the opinion that the indignation caused by the efforts of the Federalist members of the House to defeat the well known wishes of the country, in the election of 1801, had a greater effect in one week in bringing the great body of the Federalists into [sympathy] with his election than could have been effected by years of mild and impartial administration. Whatever the cause, the prompt ratification of the amendment by the States showed their realization of the necessity for such a measure.

The Ratification Process in the States

As soon as the final vote was taken in Congress the amendment was sent to the Governors of the States. Before the next month brought in the New Year five States had responded. Kentucky had given her assent; Virginia ratified with only one dissenting voice in the House; North Carolina had no opposition in the Senate and but eighteen negative votes in the House of Commons. In Maryland there was some opposition from the Federalists in the House, but none in the Senate in the ratification on December 30th, and Ohio fulfilled by prompt ratification the expectation of Governor Tiffin who had recommended the measure in his message. A few days afterwards, January 7, 1804, Pennsylvania followed suit. In Vermont there was some heated discussion growing out of the fact that Mr. Elliot, who had been the organ of the House in submitting to Congress their desire to amend the Constitution, offered a letter assigning his reasons for the vote he had given against the measure. This caused a repetition of the arguments pro and con which had been given in Congress. The constitutional question of the majority by which it had passed was brought up, but to no purpose. On January 27th the Council unanimously adopted the amendment, and the House passed it by a good majority.

Delaware's Rejection

The first check to this triumphant progress was received a little before this in Delaware. January 6th the amendment was laid before the Legislature by Governor Hall, with an urgent recommendation. It was rejected and the following resolutions passed instead: "Resolved, That the amendment to the Constitution of the United States . . . be and the same hereby is disapproved by the Legislature of this State for the reasons following:

1. Because at all times innovations of the Constitution are dangerous, but more especially when the changes are dictated by party spirit, are designed for temporary purposes and calculated to accomplish personal views.

2. Because as representatives of a small State we are sensible that in the nature of things every change in the Constitution will be in favor of the large States who will never be disposed to allow and will always have the means to prevent a variation favorable to the interests of the small States.

3. Because, in fact, the proposed amendment does reduce the power and weight of the small States, in the case provided by the Constitution for the choice of President by the House of Representatives, by limiting the selection to three instead of five candidates having the greatest number of electoral votes.

4. Because the present mode of election gives to the small States a control and weight in the election of President which are destroyed by the contemplated amendment.

5. Because it is the true and permanent interest of a free people among whom the relations of a majority and a minority must ever be fluctuating, to maintain the just weight and respectability of the minority, by every proper provision, not impeaching the principle that the majority ought to govern; and we consider the present mode of election as calculated to repress the natural intolerance of a majority and to secure some consideration and forebearance in relation to the minority.

6. Because we view the existing provision in the Constitution as among the wisest of its regulations. History furnishes many examples of nations, and particularly of

republics, in their delirious devotion to individuals, being ready to sacrifice their liberties and dearest rights to the personal aggrandizement of their idol. The existing regulation furnishes some check to this human infirmity by the occasional power given to a few to negative the will of the majority as to one man, leaving them every other qualified citizen in the country for the range of their selection.

7. Because we are not satisfied that the said amendment has constitutionally passed the two houses of Congress; the Constitution requiring the concurrence of two-thirds of both houses, which in a case of such magnitude and designed precaution must be considered as two-thirds of the entire number composing the two houses; whereas, it appears that the said amendment is not supported by the concurrence of two-thirds of the whole number of either house."

The Last States

In February, Rhode Island ratified by a unanimous vote in the Senate and a vote of 42 to 18 in the House. In a letter from Senator Butler, of South Carolina, to the Governor of that State, he said that Governor Fenner of Rhode Island was opposed to the amendment, but some Federalists opposing it also, the Republicans said it must be a good thing, so pushed it through. During the same month Governor Clinton laid the amendment before the New York Legislature, and it was agreed to without a division in the Senate and by a large majority in the House. New Jersey, also, in the month of February, sent in her ratification.

The second State to reject the amendment was Massachusetts. Governor Strong, in his presentation, neither recommended nor condemned it, but the answer of the House gave an indication of what its fate would be. They said they would pursue the discussion of the subject "under impressions of the highest respect and veneration for an instrument so valuable as the Constitution of the United States, the deliberate production of our first and long tried patriots, united with our most enlightened and experienced statesmen." It was said during the debates that it was "high time for a 'union of all honest men' to oppose consolidation and appear as champions of the small States." On February 2d, the amendment was rejected in the Senate, and the next day by the House. Connecticut followed the example of Massachusetts and rejected it on May 24th, by a strict party vote.

In Georgia, Governor Milledge called a special session of the Legislature, which met at Louisville on May 4th, and ratified it unanimously. A special session seems to have been called in South Carolina also, and Governor Richardson cited the events of the last election as an argument for ratification. He enclosed two letters from Senator Butler, giving his reasons for voting against the amendment, and urging South Carolina to reject it as a question, not of party politics, but of State rights. In spite of this protest the Legislature ratified it.

In New Hampshire the question had been brought up in January but was postponed until June. When it was again taken up, it passed the Senate and the House, but the Governor vetoed it as if it had been an ordinary bill. The Legislature passed it again, but with the same vote, which was not the two-thirds majority called for by the State Constitution to override the Governor's veto. Though the Republicans of the State considered that the Governor had no part in the ratification of an amendment and that the State had given its voice in favor of this one, New Hampshire was not included in the official list of ratifying States.

The last State to pass upon the question was Tennessee, which, on July 27th, ratified with perfect unanimity in both Houses. Thus of the seventeen States, thirteen, not including New Hampshire, had voted for the amendment, and this being the requisite three-fourths, on September 25, 1804, the

Secretary of State issued a proclamation declaring it in force. The election of 1804–1805 was held in accordance with its provisions.

Fixing a Broken Election Process

Akhil Reed Amar

Akhil Reed Amar graduated from Yale College and Yale Law School. He has taught at Yale Law School since 1985. He has written many times on constitutional issues for the New York Times, *the* Los Angeles Times, *and the* Washington Post. *He also authored the book* The Bill of Rights: Creation and Reconstruction *(1998). Akhil describes how the Twelfth Amendment remedied a flaw in how electors voted for president and vice president. Beyond simply fixing a problem with the voting, the Twelfth Amendment radically altered the presidency, vice presidency, and political parties as the result of its ratification.*

Through its seemingly small modifications of the original electoral college, the Twelfth Amendment in fact worked rather large changes in the basic structure of the American presidency and its relation to other parts of the American constitutional order. First, by knowingly facilitating the efforts of political parties to run presidential–vice presidential tickets—tickets likely to be linked to slates of local and congressional candidates—the amendment paved the way for increased involvement of ordinary citizens in the presidential-selection process. Even if an ordinary voter did not know the presidential candidates directly, he could with relative ease learn about party ideologies and traditions. He could also make plausible inferences about each party's presidential candidate by directly assessing that party's local candidates, whom he *was* well positioned to know personally or with one degree of separation. In 1800, the last presidential election held under the Philadelphia plan, only one-third of the states allowed

Akhil Reed Amar, *America's Constitution.* New York: Random House, 2005. Copyright © 2005 by Akhil Reed Amar. All rights reserved. Reproduced by permission of Random House, Inc.

voters to pick electors directly. In 1804, the first election under the amendment, this number doubled. By 1828, voters were directly choosing electors in twenty-one of the twenty-four states.

Alongside the increased informal role for ordinary voters would come a decreased formal role for Congress in the presidential-selection process. By eliminating double-ballot rules apt to create electoral-college deadlocks and misfires, the Twelfth Amendment lessened the likelihood that any given presidential election would be decided by Congress. The new system would thus work to enhance the executive's formal independence from the legislature. After its dramatic selection of [Thomas] Jefferson over [Aaron] Burr, Congress would be called upon to act in only two of the ensuing fifty presidential contests—directly in 1824–25 and indirectly in 1876–77.

The Twelfth Amendment Changed the Vice Presidency

The Twelfth Amendment also helped shape a new kind of vice president, a rather diminished figure compared to his Philadelphia-plan predecessor. Under Article II, the vice president was supposed to be a genuinely presidential personage, a statesman who had in fact received the second-highest vote total for the presidency itself. Under the amendment, the vice presidency would instead go to a man who no elector had picked—and that perhaps no elector would pick—for the top job. The Philadelphia plan had undeniably generated vice presidents of stature in the persons of [John] Adams and Jefferson, twin giants of the American Revolution who would each go on to become president in his own right. . . .

Most important of all, the Twelfth Amendment sired a new kind of president, apt to be far more openly populist and partisan than his predecessors. Modeling himself as an American version of [Henry St. John] Bolingbroke's fabled Patriot King, [George] Washington had tried to stand as a man above party, with [Alexander] Hamilton as his right hand and Jefferson as his left. (Republican critics complained that in practice, he had often favored his right hand.) In the Age of [Andrew] Jackson, however, Washington's initial effort to embody a president above party would decisively give way to a more modern model of the president as an avowed party leader. Though the Twelfth Amendment did not compel this shift, it plainly enabled it.

In the words of one early expert on the Twelfth Amendment, Lolabel House, "The enormous consequence of [the amendment] has been to make party government constitutional." A more recent book by Tadahisa Kuroda, *The Origins of the Twelfth Amendment*, seconds this assessment: "The amendment modifying the electoral college had a partisan motive and in effect recognized the existence of national political parties." ...

The Twelfth Amendment and Its Effects on States and Slavery

The Twelfth Amendment also gave the nation a more visibly and undeniably slavocratic presidential-selection system than the one that America had ratified in the late 1780s. In 1803, it could not be persuasively argued that Article II's rules had in fact worked to boost small states. In the four presidential elections that had taken place thus far, the rules had thrice crowned a man from the largest state (in electoral votes) and once anointed a man from the second-largest state. The runner-up slot had also gone to a big-state man every time. Six of the seven largest states (in free population, circa 1800) had sent men to the executive cabinet, while only one of the ten smallest states had done so.

The Twelfth Amendment itself, by both omission and commission, would only compound the big-state advantage, as was repeatedly emphasized during congressional debate over the measure. After 1800 it was evident both that any state seeking to maximize its clout had to select a statewide slate of electors, winner-take-all, and also that under a general regime of state-winner-take-all, big states would enjoy an advantage. Though prominent proposals had surfaced after 1801 to require states to renounce winner-take-all systems, the framers of the Twelfth Amendment spurned all such proposals and instead increased the big-state advantage in two distinct ways. First, the Amendment's separate ballots for presidents and vice presidents reduced the likelihood of an electoral-vote tie between running mates and thus increased the odds that elections would be decided by the electors themselves (in a system favoring big states) rather than in the House (operating on a one-state, one-vote rule). Second, in the event no presidential candidate had an electoral-vote majority, the House could choose only among the top three vote-getters, rather than among the top five. This, too, shrank the domain over which the state-equality principle would operate.

Several congressmen attacked the amendment for its obvious weakening of the influence of small states, and tiny Delaware in fact refused to ratify the amendment on these grounds. However, by 1803 politically savvy Americans had come to see that the nation's deepest fissures ran not between big states and small states, but rather between free states and slave states. Every actual combination of president and vice president (and indeed every losing ticket as well) had balanced a Northerner and a Southerner. . . .

The election of 1800–01 had also drawn the nation's attention, in the most dramatic fashion possible, to the Philadelphia plan's proslavery bias. In 1787–89, many Northern ratifiers had failed to understand the full significance of the words "three fifths." Refighting the last war, they had focused more on apportioning taxes than on allocating House members and presidential electors. But by 1803, everyone understood that virtually no revenue would come from direct taxes subject to the three-fifths clause. (Only once, in 1798, had a small direct tax been levied.) By contrast, the hard-fought and razor-close election of 1800–01 had made the three-fifths clause's electoral significance obvious to anyone with eyes and a brain.

For without the added electoral votes created by the existence of Southern slaves, John Adams would have won the election of 1800—as everyone at the time plainly understood. Jefferson's (and Burr's) electors came from states that had a smaller total free population than the states whose electors backed Adams. Had the electoral college been apportioned on the basis of free population—with no three-fifths bonus—Jefferson would have ended up with about four electoral votes less than Adams rather than eight votes more. As one New England paper sharply put the point, Jefferson was riding "into the TEMPLE OF LIBERTY, upon the *shoulders of slaves*.". . .

In short, whereas Article II originally created the presidency in the image of George Washington, Amendment XII refashioned the office in the likeness of Thomas Jefferson and in a manner that prefigured Andrew Jackson. After the adoption of this amendment, America's presidential-election rules—and thus America's presidents—would generally be more democratic, more partisan, and more openly slavocratic. Prior to the amendment, America's first president had taken steps to free his slaves, and America's second president had none who needed freeing. America's third president—a transitional figure elected under Article II and re-elected under Amendment XII—had passionately condemned slavery in his early years but did rather little to back up his youthful rhetoric after his slavery-supported triumph in 1801. The next dozen presidents—mostly Southern slaveholders or Northern doughfaces [Northerners who supported slavery]—likewise did little to challenge slavery.

CONSTITUTIONAL
AMENDMENTS
BEYOND THE BILL OF RIGHTS

CHAPTER 2

Testing the Twelfth Amendment

The Election of 1804

Gaye Wilson

In the following article Gaye Wilson discusses how the Constitution set up a system that could lead to a split vote between a president and his vice presidential running mate. However, the Twelfth Amendment was eventually ratified to prevent such a situation as happened in the election of 1800 from occurring again. After the Twelfth Amendment was ratified, it was put to the test in the presidential election of 1804 between incumbent president Thomas Jefferson and his challenger Charles Pinckney. Gaye Wilson, a research historian at the Robert H. Smith International Center for Jefferson Studies, has lectured and published essays on Thomas Jefferson.

Before the election of 1804, President Thomas Jefferson projected that his party would carry all but four of the 17 states in the fall balloting. It did even better. The Jeffersonian Republicans defeated the Federalists everywhere except Connecticut and Delaware, thus giving Jefferson the presidency for another four years.

Jefferson Reviews His First Administration

Jefferson accounted for the overwhelming support at the polls in his second inaugural address by reviewing his administration's first-term achievements. Early in his remarks he stated: "On taking this station ... I declared the principles on which I believed it my duty to administer the affairs of our commonwealth. My conscience tells me that I have, on every occasion, acted up to that declaration."

Gaye Wilson, "In a Landslide, Jefferson Wins a Second Term," *Monticello Newsletter*, vol. 15, Winter 2004, pp. 1–5. Copyright © Thomas Jefferson Foundation, Inc., 2004. Reproduced by permission.

He went on to note that foreign relations were improved and internal taxes discontinued. He said that import taxes, "paid cheerfully by those who can afford to add foreign luxuries to domestic comforts," supported a smaller national government, allowed for the expansion of the nation through the purchase of Louisiana and Indian territories, and reduced the national debt.

Jefferson elaborated upon the topic of Louisiana, as the purchase treaty was regarded as an outstanding achievement of his administration. "Is it not better," he asked, "that the opposite bank of the Mississippi should be settled by our own brethren and children, than by strangers of another family? With which shall we be most likely to live in harmony and friendly intercourse?"

Jefferson did not, however, forgo the partisan opportunity to remind the public that "the acquisition of Louisiana has been disapproved by some." Most Federalists had openly opposed the purchase. Based primarily in New England and determined to protect that region's trade and shipping interests, the Federalists were uneasy with the country's westward movement and the growing importance of the port of New Orleans. But to Jefferson, the 1804 election victory sounded the approval of his western vision by the majority of Americans.

The Problem of Burr

The achievements of Jefferson's first term had assured that he would be re-nominated by his party. But the Republican caucus, which met in February 1804, had dropped the Vice President Aaron Burr in favor of New York's governor, George Clinton, as Jefferson's running mate.

Burr had lost the confidence of many Republicans during the drawn-out election of 1800. In that contest, Jefferson, then vice president, defeated the Federalist incumbent, John Adams. But because the Republicans had failed to make sure at least one electoral vote for vice presidential candidate Burr

The third president of the United States, Thomas Jefferson, served from 1801 to 1809. ©
Bettmann/Corbis.

was withheld, Jefferson and Burr tied for the presidency. The
contest went to the House of Representatives, where Federal-

ists seized the opportunity to block Jefferson's election by giving their votes to Burr. The deadlock was not broken until mid-February 1801, when the House elected Jefferson on its 36th ballot.

Because Burr did not withdraw his name from contention for the presidency, Jefferson and other Republicans came to doubt his loyalty and were uneasy with his holding a position of national prominence. As Jefferson began organizing his administration, he ignored Burr's patronage recommendations and did not consult him on policy decisions.

In 1804, aware that he would not be a part of the national ticket, Burr challenged the Republicans in his home state of New York by running for governor. The Federalists considered supporting Burr to create greater division among the Republicans, but Federalist leader Alexander Hamilton spoke out strongly against Burr, and others asked, "Is he to be used by the Federalists, or is he a two-edged sword, that must not be drawn?"

Burr lost the New York election in the spring of 1804, and cast much of the blame on Hamilton—one factor that led to their famous duel in July of that year. Hamilton's death was considered the death of Burr's political career as well, yet he returned to Washington to complete his term as vice president. President Jefferson completely divorced himself from Burr, saying, "There never had been an intimacy between us, and but little association."

The Twelfth Amendment

The Jeffersonian Republicans could rid themselves of Burr, but that did not address the problem inherent in the electoral process that had produced the tie vote of 1800. The Constitution allowed each elector two votes but did not require that they be designated for president and vice president. Thus, the candidate with the most votes would become president, the runner-up vice president. In light of the development of partisan political parties, this was recognized as problematic, and in the first session of Congress following the election Jeffersonians led the move to amend the Constitution.

Support crossed party lines but was far from unanimous. The legislation was not passed by both houses until December 1803. The proposal sent to the states for ratification specified that as electors met in their respective states, "they shall name in their ballots the person voted for as President, and in distinct ballots the person voted for as Vice-President."

As any change to the Constitution required ratification by three-fourths of the states, Jefferson and Secretary of State James Madison left Washington for the summer recess with the electoral process still undecided. Madison assured Jefferson that all was ready "for giving effect to the proposed amendment." But it was not until Sept. 25, 1804, that Madison was able to declare that the 12th Amendment to the Constitution had been ratified.

The Election of 1804

In keeping with the practice of the time, Jefferson and his Federalist rival, Charles Cotesworth Pinckney of South Carolina (who had been Adams' running mate in 1800), abstained from any overt campaigning. Both relied instead upon their party machinery working at the grassroots level and through the press.

The strongest opposition to Jefferson was based in New England. Federalist William Plumer of New Hampshire lamented that Jefferson and his supporters were even allowed to call themselves "republican," believing "Democrats and Jacobins" far more appropriate. Plumer authored six newspaper articles under the pseudonym Cato in which he went through Jefferson's political career from secretary of state to the presidency and even referenced Jefferson's one published book, *Notes on the State of Virginia*, to outline what he saw as Jefferson's inconsistencies.

Despite these efforts, Plumer had to record in his personal journal entry for Feb. 13, 1805, his party's overwhelming loss. When the electoral ballots were counted that day before a joint session of Congress, Jefferson and Clinton received 162 votes apiece while Pinckney and his running mate, Rufus King of New York, had 14 apiece. It was none other than Aaron Burr, sitting as presiding officer of the Senate, who declared that Thomas Jefferson had been elected president and George Clinton vice president.

Jefferson had run for re-election to affirm the nation's approval. He wrote in January 1804: "The abominable slanders of my political enemies have obliged me to call for that verdict from my country in the only way it can be obtained." He concluded that a favorable vote would be "my sufficient voucher to the rest of the world and to posterity, and leave me free to seek, at a definite time, the repose I sincerely wished to have retired to now."

Certainly the election of 1804 gave validation to Jefferson and the direction set by his administration. It would prove to be the apex of his political career, as the accomplishments of his first term would not be matched in his second. Escalating wars in Europe would threaten American neutrality and damage the prosperity experienced by the nation during Jefferson's first term. He would come to experience an observation on the presidency he had offered many years before, "that no man will ever bring out of that office the reputation which carries him into it."

Ray v. Blair: Political Parties Can Require Electors to Vote for Their Party's Nominee

Stanley Reed

The question before the U.S. Supreme Court was whether a state political party could require its presidential electors to vote only for that party's nominee for president. This meant that only electors who promised the state party that they would vote according to how they were instructed would be acceptable and allowed to cast the electoral votes for their state in the electoral college. The U.S. Supreme Court sided with the state parties and ruled that the Twelfth Amendment does not prohibit political parties from requiring that electors must vote for their candidate. Justice Stanley Reed delivered the opinion of the court. He served as an associate justice from 1938 to 1957.

Where a state authorizes a political party to choose its nominees for Presidential Electors in a state-controlled party primary election and to fix the qualifications for the candidates, it is not violative of the Federal Constitution for the party to require the candidates for the office of Presidential Elector to take a pledge to support the nominees of the party's National Convention for President and Vice-President or for the party's officers to refuse to certify as a candidate for Presidential Elector a person otherwise qualified who refuses to take such a pledge.

Overall Findings

1. Presidential Electors exercise a federal function in balloting for President and Vice-President, but they are not

Ray v. Blair, 343 U.S. 214 (1952) U.S. Supreme Court, 1952. http://caselaw.lp.find law.com/scripts/getcase.pl?court=us&vol=343&invol=214.

federal officers. They act by authority of the state which in turn receives its authority from the Federal Constitution.

2. Exclusion of a candidate in a party primary by a state or political party because such candidate will not pledge to support the party's nominees is a method of securing party candidates in the general election who are pledged to the philosophy and leadership of that party; and it is an exercise of the state's right . . . to appoint electors in such manner as it may choose. . . .

3. The Twelfth Amendment does not bar a political party from requiring of a candidate for Presidential Elector in its primary a pledge to support the nominees of its National Convention. . . .

Background

MR. JUSTICE REED delivered the opinion of the Court.

The Supreme Court of Alabama upheld a peremptory writ of mandamus [a commandment from a higher court to a lower one] requiring the petitioner, the chairman of that state's Executive Committee of the Democratic Party, to certify respondent Edmund Blair, a member of that party, to the Secretary of State of Alabama as a candidate for Presidential Elector in the Democratic Primary to be held May 6, 1952. Respondent Blair was admittedly qualified as a candidate except that he refused to include the following quoted words in the pledge required of party candidates—a pledge to aid and support "the nominees of the National Convention of the Democratic Party for President and Vice-President of the United States." The chairman's refusal of certification was based on that omission.

The mandamus was approved on the sole ground that the above requirement restricted the freedom of a federal elector to vote in his Electoral College for his choice for President.

The pledge was held void as unconstitutional under the Twelfth Amendment of the Constitution of the United States. . . .

The Primary

As is well known, political parties in the modern sense were not born with the Republic. They were created by necessity, by the need to organize the rapidly increasing population, scattered over our Land, so as to coordinate efforts to secure needed legislation and oppose that deemed undesirable. The party conventions of locally chosen delegates, from the county to the national level, succeeded the caucuses of self-appointed legislators or other interested individuals. Dissatisfaction with the manipulation of conventions caused that system to be largely superseded by the direct primary. This was particularly true in the South because, with the predominance of the Democratic Party in that section, the nomination was more important than the election. There primaries are generally, as in Alabama, optional. Various tests of party allegiance for candidates in direct primaries are found in a number of states. The requirement of a pledge from the candidate participating in primaries to support the nominee is not unusual. Such a provision protects a party from intrusion by those with adverse political principles. It was under the authority of 347 of the Alabama Code, note 2, . . . that the State Democratic Executive Committee of Alabama adopted a resolution on January 26, 1952, requiring candidates in its primary to pledge support to the nominees of the National Convention of the Democratic Party for President and Vice-President. It is this provision in the qualifications required by the party under 347 which the Supreme Court of Alabama held unconstitutional in this case.

The opinion of the Supreme Court of Alabama concluded that the Executive Committee requirement violated the Twelfth Amendment, note 1. . . . It said:

"We appreciate the argument that from time immemorial, the electors selected to vote in the college have voted in accordance with the wishes of the party to which they belong. But in doing so, the effective compulsion has been party loyalty. That theory has generally been taken for granted, so that the voting for a president and vice-president has been usually formal merely. But the Twelfth Amendment does not make it so. The nominees of the party for president and vice-president may have become disqualified, or peculiarly offensive not only to the electors but their constituents also. They should be free to vote for another, as contemplated by the Twelfth Amendment." . . .

Opposing Argument

The argument against the party's power to exclude as candidates in the primary those unwilling to agree to aid and support the national nominees runs as follows: The constitutional method for the selection of the President and Vice-President is for states to appoint electors who shall in turn vote for our chief executives. The intention of the Founders was that those electors should exercise their judgment in voting for President and Vice-President. Therefore this requirement of a pledge is a restriction in substance, if not in form, that interferes with the performance of this constitutional duty to select the proper persons to head the Nation, according to the best judgment of the elector. . . .

In Alabama, too, the primary and general elections are a part of the state-controlled elective process. The issue here, however, is quite different from the power of Congress to punish criminal conduct in a primary or to allow damages for wrongs to rights secured by the Constitution. A state's or a political party's exclusion of candidates from a party primary because they will not pledge to support the party's nominees is a method of securing party candidates in the general election, pledged to the philosophy and leadership of that party. It is an exercise of the state's right to appoint electors in such manner, subject to possible constitutional limitations, as it may choose. The fact that the primary is a part of the election machinery is immaterial unless the requirement of pledge violates some constitutional or statutory provision. . . .

Secondly, we consider the argument that the Twelfth Amendment demands absolute freedom for the elector to vote his own choice, uninhibited by a pledge. It is true that the Amendment says the electors shall vote by ballot. But it is also true that the Amendment does not prohibit an elector's announcing his choice beforehand, pledging himself. The suggestion that in the early elections candidates for electors—contemporaries of the Founders—would have hesitated, because of constitutional limitations, to pledge themselves to support party nominees in the event of their selection as electors is impossible to accept. History teaches that the electors were expected to support the party nominees. Experts in the history of government recognize the long-standing practice. Indeed, more than twenty states do not print the names of the candidates for electors on the general election ballot. Instead, in one form or another, they allow a vote for the presidential candidate of the national conventions to be counted as a vote for his party's nominees for the electoral college. This long-continued practical interpretation of the constitutional propriety of an implied or oral pledge of his ballot by a candidate for elector as to his vote in the electoral college weighs heavily in considering the constitutionality of a pledge, such as the one here required, in the primary. . . .

We conclude that the Twelfth Amendment does not bar a political party from requiring the pledge to support the nominees of the National Convention. Where a state authorizes a party to choose its nominees for elector in a party primary and to fix the qualifications for the candidates, we see no federal constitutional objection to the requirement of this pledge.

Electors Can Vote Faithlessly

Robert W. Bennett

Robert W. Bennett is a former dean of the School of Law at Northwestern University and has been a member of the faculty since 1969. He has also served as president of the American Bar Foundation. In addition to holding those positions, he has published such books as Talking It Through: Puzzles of American Democracy *(2003) and* Taming the Electoral College *(2006). Bennett tackles the notion of "faithless electors" and whether they could upset the election process for president. He does this by discussing what a "faithless elector" is, the history of "faithless electors," and the potential for future problems with such an electoral system.*

While there was a bit of suspense on election night of 2004, by the next morning it was clear that George Bush had secured reelection, no ifs, ands, or buts. Or was it? The electoral college was not to meet (in fifty-one separate state and District of Columbia gatherings) until the Monday after the second Wednesday in December, some forty-one days later. Suppose at those electoral college proceedings, a majority of the electors had cast their votes not for George Bush, as they had been committed to do beforehand, but for Utah's Senator Robert Bennett (or, for that matter, anyone else who was a natural born citizen of the United States, at least thirty-five years old, and had been resident in the United States for the prior fourteen years), even though not a single popular vote in the entire nation had been cast for Bennett. That, of course, did not happen, and there was never any real chance of it happening. But what if it had happened? Would George

Robert W. Bennett, "The Problem of the Faithless Elector: Trouble Aplenty Brewing Just Below the Surface in Choosing the President," *Northwestern University Law Review*, vol. 100, 2006, pp. 121–127, 129–130. Copyright © 2006 by Northwestern University, School of Law. Reproduced by permission.

North Dakota's electors—former governor Ed Schafer (left), former state senator Bryce Streibel, and lieutenant governor Rosemarie Myrdal—certify their votes for the electoral college during the 2000 presidential election. AP Images.

Bush or Robert Bennett—or perhaps neither—be our president? That is the problem, in its starkest form, of the "faithless" elector.

Some states have statutory provisions that explicitly purport to "bind" electors to vote in accord with their prior commitments. These laws sometimes simply instruct electors to vote as committed, but sometimes they provide penalties of one sort or another. North Carolina, for instance, imposes a fine of $500 for faithlessness, while New Mexico makes it a "fourth degree felony." Some laws require political parties to extract pledges, while others have state officers compose and administer oaths of faithfulness. And some states provide that a faithless vote constitutes resignation from the office of elector.

If these laws purport to change faithless votes, however, they may be unavailing. In the 1952 decision *Ray v. Blair*, the Supreme Court held that states may allow political parties to extract pledges of faithfulness to the nominee of the national party from candidates for elector who seek to run in the party's primary. But the court explicitly reserved the possibility that the pledge was "legally unenforceable because of an assumed constitutional freedom." A whole host of electoral college commentators insists that electors have just such a "constitutional freedom" to vote faithlessly. . . .

Recent Faithless Electors

While no president has ever come to office through the votes of faithless electors, one faithless elector abstained in the presidential balloting in the 2000 election, while in 2004 another elector in a different state voted for John Edwards for president, rather than John Kerry. Over the years there have been perhaps a dozen faithless electors of one stripe or another in the presidential contests. And, at least in the close 2000 election, there is nothing at all fanciful about the possibility that faithless electors might have changed the outcome. Even after the Florida contest was decided in George Bush's favor that year, if three Republican electors had (successfully) voted for Albert Gore—but all other electors had remained faithful to their pre-election commitments—Gore would have triumphed in the electoral college, 270–268. . . .

Problems with Faithless Electors

If the 2000 election had been decided by faithless electors— either way—the result would have held great peril for the nation. To all appearances, the modern electoral college is one in which each state conducts a popular election among presidential candidates. The state's allocation of electors—one for each member of the House and Senate, and effectively three for the District of Columbia—is then awarded on the basis of the outcome in the state. The electoral college winner is the candidate who secures a majority of the total number of electors. At least in a two-person race, short of an electoral college tie there seems to be no room for ambiguity about the result.

States that by Law Bind Electors to Vote for the State's Popular Vote-getter for the Office of President	States that Do Not Legally Bind Electors to Vote for the State's Popular Vote-getter for the Office of President
Alabama	Arizona
Alaska	Arkansas
California	Delaware
Colorado	Georgia
Connecticut	Idaho
District of Columbia	Illinois
Florida	Indiana
Hawaii	Iowa
Maine	Kansas
Maryland	Kentucky
Massachusetts	Louisiana
Michigan	Minnesota
Mississippi	Missouri
Montana	New Hampshire
Nebraska	New Jersey
Nevada	New York
New Mexico	North Dakota
North Carolina	Pennsylvania
Ohio	Rhode Island
Oklahoma	Tennessee
Oregon	Texas
South Carolina	Utah
Vermont	West Virginia
Virginia	
Washington	
Wisconsin	
Wyoming	

TAKEN FROM: Office of the Federal Register

That is why on the morning after election day in 2004 George Bush was understood to have won—no ifs, ands, or buts. . . .

Given this modern understanding, widespread social turmoil, even widespread violence, could well result if an election result was altered by faithless electors. While electoral votes are cast about forty days after the election, the votes are not formally counted for another three weeks or so, at a joint meeting of the House and Senate. At that meeting, the validity of elector faithlessness would, no doubt, be challenged, and the legitimacy of that challenge might be challenged as well. Particularly if the two houses were controlled by different political parties, the outcome of the struggle could remain uncertain for a long time, with unforeseeable results. The Supreme Court might get into the fray, as it did in the 2000 election, but there is no guaranteeing that the joint meeting would accede to a court decision, particularly if the court decision favored a candidate of a party that was in the minority in both houses. After all, the Constitution says that the joint meeting is where the votes "shall . . . be counted." One venerable commentator [Albert Rosenthal] has said that "the . . . dispute over the legitimacy of the election of a new President [where faithless electors played a role] might well inflict grave injuries upon the nation." That is, perhaps, to put it mildly. Is it not possible, for instance, that foreign enemies would confront the United States in the atmosphere of uncertainty that could prevail? Even if that did not happen, and even if some settlement of the election dispute was reached with expedition, there would likely be bitterness and dissension in many quarters, and for a very long time. The poisoned atmosphere would make the unhappiness with the 2000 election seem like child's play.

How Faithless Electors Came About

Just how have we come to this pass? Perhaps we can begin to understand the polar possibilities for electoral legitimacy by noting a touch of irony in use of the word "faithless" to describe electors who defect from their pre-election commitments. As originally envisaged, electors were to be independent decisionmakers, "men," in Alexander Hamilton's words, "most capable of analyzing the qualities adapted to the station and acting under circumstances favorable to deliberation, and to a judicious combination of all the reasons and inducements which were proper to govern their choice." They were to deliberate and then exercise discretion to come up with the best person(s) for the job of president. Indeed, it is hard to see why the office of elector would have been created in the first place if no real process of choice attended the office. For this reason, today's faithless elector might actually be rather faithful to the original conception of his assignment.

The seemingly awkward choice of separate state meetings for the electors seems to have derived some of its appeal as helping to assure this independence of electors. Separate meetings of each state's electors might be seen as a device for assuring that bargaining would not insinuate itself into the selection process. The "detached and divided situation" of the electors, as Hamilton put it, would expose them much less to "heats and ferments." With no knowledge of the deliberations of the other electoral college delegations, each group of electors could ask and answer for itself the question of just who in the country could rise above the battle of interests, who would best answer the call of being an executive not for one faction, nor even for an amalgam of many, but for the entire nation. This is what leads to the claim . . . of constitutional protection for elector discretion.

If elector faithlessness can be traced in this fashion to the original constitutional design, it is astounding how quickly many of the assumptions on which it was based proved to be false. Even while many clung to a view of politics in general as rising above factions in the search for the common good, ferocious differences surfaced almost immediately about just what the "true interest" of the new republic was, and the multiplicity of interests and sentiments coalesced around two large-scale groupings characterized by a great deal of mutual distrust. Political parties, nowhere mentioned in the Constitution, quickly became the organizing media of politics, and almost immediately reached not only into the legislature but into the electoral college mechanism for selecting the president as well. Electors increasingly came to think of themselves as agents of political parties rather than as engaged in deliberation about who in the nation might best serve as a wise president above factional politics. And with political parties as instruments of political coordination and communication, cooperation among the various state electoral college delegations could proceed before the simultaneous far-flung meetings of those delegations. . . .

The Electoral College and Electors Today

These various developments have produced a modern conception of the electoral college that bears scant resemblance to what those who devised it had in mind. It is dominated by popular election of electors, which is not inconsistent with what the constitutional framers envisaged, but is not required by that vision either. However chosen, the electoral college is not made up of discretion-laden electors, as the framers intended. Political parties are central to its operation, rather than absent—or at best peripheral—as the framers hoped and expected. The separate state meetings are not the disconnected deliberations they envisaged, but rather staged and coordinated proceedings orchestrated by those same political parties. The only respect in which the modern electoral college resembles what the constitutional framers had in mind is the allocation of electoral voting strength by states. And even that has been importantly transformed by near-universal state adoption of winner-take-all rules for awarding a state's electoral votes.

The assumption of elector faithfulness appeared very early. In 1796 Samuel Miles's vote for Thomas Jefferson despite his prior commitment to the Federalist candidate John Adams elicited the following response from an aggrieved Federalist: "What, do I chuse Samuel Miles to determine for me whether John Adams or Thomas Jefferson shall be President? No! I chuse him to *act*, not *think*." James Russell Lowell, elected as a Republican elector in the contentious 1876 election, made the same point from the other side of the relationship of voter to elector. Urged to vote for the Democrat (and nationwide popular vote winner) Tilden, he declined, saying,

> I have no choice, and am bound in honor to vote for [the Republican] Hayes, as the people who chose me expected me to do. They did not choose me because they had confidence in my judgment, but because they thought they knew what that judgment would be.... It is a plain question of trust.

Over the years this assumption of elector reliability has come to go without saying, as the form of the ballots ... silently, but dramatically, attests. Just as surely, however, the possibility of elector faithlessness persists, hiding in the shadows of the process. This is a mischievous mix that we would do well to resolve before rather than after we find ourselves embroiled in damaging controversy.

Jones v. Bush: Challenging the Residency Restrictions of the Twelfth Amendment

Stephen E. Jones et al. v. Governor George W. Bush et al.

*This court case was set up by the Twelfth Amendment's require-
ment that if both the presidential and vice presidential candidates are from the same home state, then that state's electors
cannot vote for the two of them. Therefore, petitioners were try-
ing to prevent George W. Bush and Dick Cheney from receiving
Texas's electoral votes due to their arguments that both Bush's
and Cheney's home state was Texas.*

This is an action by three Texas registered voters who allege
that Richard B. Cheney ("Secretary Cheney" [Cheney was
formerly U.S. secretary of defense]), nominee of the Republican Party for Vice President of the United States, is an "inhabitant" of the state of Texas, and that under the Twelfth Amendment to the United States Constitution, members of the
Electoral College from the state of Texas ("Texas Electors") are
prohibited from voting for both Governor George W. Bush
("Governor Bush") for the office of President of the United
States and for Secretary Cheney for the office of Vice President. Plaintiffs seek a preliminary injunction to prevent the
Texas Electors from casting their votes in favor of both Governor Bush and Secretary Cheney. Defendants move to dismiss,
contending that plaintiffs lack standing, that their suit presents a non-justiciable political question, and that they have
failed to state a claim on which relief can be granted. Because
plaintiffs do not have standing to sue, the court grants

Stephen E. Jones et al. v. Governor George W. Bush et al., in United States District
Court for the Northern District of Texas Dallas Division, December, 2000, pp. 1–6, 8,
10–13.

defendants' motion to dismiss. Given the importance of entering a ruling that will assist the parties in obtaining full appellate review in the short period that remains before the Electoral College votes on December 18, 2000, the court reaches the merits of plaintiffs' preliminary injunction application and denies it. The court holds that plaintiffs have failed to show a substantial likelihood of success on their contention that Secretary Cheney has been at some point since July 21, 2000, or will be on December 18, 2000, an inhabitant of the state of Texas, within the meaning of the Twelfth Amendment.

The Twelfth Amendment provides, in relevant part:

> The Electors shall meet in their respective states, and vote by ballot for President and Vice-President, one of whom, at least, shall not be an inhabitant of the same state with themselves[.]

The Argument of the Plaintiffs

Plaintiffs sue Governor Bush, Secretary Cheney, and the 32 Texas Electors, contending that, under the Twelfth Amendment, the Texas Electors may not vote for Governor Bush for the office of President of the United States and for Secretary Cheney for the office of Vice President of the United States because both are inhabitants of the state of Texas. In their first claim for relief, plaintiffs seek a judgment under 28 U.S.C. § 2201 declaring *inter alia* [among other things] that the 32 electoral votes of the Texas Electors may not be cast for both Governor Bush and Secretary Cheney. In their second claim for relief, plaintiffs seek a preliminary injunction enjoining the Texas Electors from casting their votes in the Electoral College on December 18, 2000 in favor of both Governor Bush and Secretary Cheney, and enjoining all defendants from permitting any of the Electors to cast any of their votes in favor of either Governor Bush and Secretary Cheney, or from certifying to the United States Congress, Texas Secretary of State, or any other person, agency, media, or entity that the votes can be or were cast in their favor. . . .

Plaintiffs describe their injury from the Texas Electors' impending alleged violation of the Twelfth Amendment as a denial of "their constitutional rights." Specifically, they posit that they have "a right, as do all citizens of the United States, for the election for President and Vice-President in the Electoral College to be held in strict accordance with the Constitution of the United States and all laws governing the conduct of elections." Plaintiffs also assert a right "to protect the interests of the non-defendant candidates for President and Vice-President" who are impacted "because the votes of the defendant Electors are necessary for defendants Bush and Cheney to achieve a majority of the Electoral College." Finally, they argue that the threatened Twelfth Amendment violation infringes their right to cast a "meaningful vote." ...

Finding of the Court

Plaintiffs' assertion that a violation of the Twelfth Amendment will harm them by infringing their right to cast a meaningful vote also fails to satisfy the Article III requirement of a "distinct and palpable injury." This type of injury is necessarily abstract, and plaintiffs conspicuously fail to demonstrate how they, as opposed to the general voting population, will feel its effects. ...

Because plaintiffs have failed to demonstrate a specific and individualized injury from the impending alleged violation of the Twelfth Amendment and are unable to show personal injury through harm done to non-defendant candidates, the court holds that they do not have standing under Article III to bring this suit. The court grants defendants' motions to dismiss and dismisses this action without prejudice by judgment filed today. ...

The Key Term: "Inhabitant"

The touchstone for determining the meaning of the term "inhabitant" in the Twelfth Amendment is the intent of the Framers. Although the Twelfth Amendment was not ratified until 1804, the constitutional requirement that the President and Vice President be "inhabitants" of different states is found in the Constitution as originally adopted and ratified at the creation of the Republic. Article II, § 1, cl. 3 provided, in relevant part, that "[t]he Electors shall . . . vote by Ballot for two Persons, of whom one at least shall not be an Inhabitant of the same State with themselves." . . .

The court therefore holds that a person is an "inhabitant" of a state, within the meaning of the Twelfth Amendment, if he (1) has a physical presence within that state and (2) intends that it be his place of habitation. . . .

Cheney as Inhabitant of Wyoming

The record shows that Secretary Cheney has both a physical presence within the state of Wyoming and the intent that Wyoming be his place of habitation. It is undisputed that he was born,[1] raised, educated, and married in Wyoming and represented the state as a Member of Congress for six terms. After additional public service, he eventually moved to Dallas, Texas to become the Chief Executive Officer of Halliburton Corporation ("Halliburton").

On or about July 21, 2000 Secretary Cheney declared his intent to return to his home state of Wyoming. On or after that date, and before today, he traveled to Wyoming and registered to vote there, requested withdrawal of his Texas voter registration, voted in Wyoming in two elections, obtained a Wyoming driver's license (which, in turn, resulted in the voiding of his Texas license), and sold his Texas house. . . .

At the time the Constitution was adopted, the term "Inhabitant" was used not only in Article II, § 1, cl. 3 (and later in the Twelfth Amendment) to limit the persons for whom electors could vote for President and Vice President, but was also found in the Qualification Clauses. Article I, § 2, cl. 2 and

1. According to the vice president's Web site, Cheney was born in Lincoln, Nebraska.

Article I, § 3, cl. 3 provide, respectively, that a member of the House of Representatives and of the Senate shall be an "Inhabitant" of the State for which he is chosen. The Framers selected the term "Inhabitant" rather than "resident" because "Inhabitant" "would not exclude persons absent occasionally for a considerable time on public or private business." . . . Therefore, Secretary Cheney is not deprived of status as a Wyoming inhabitant . . . simply because he intends, if elected, to be absent from the state for a considerable time on public business.

It is evident from the preliminary injunction record that Secretary Cheney intended by his conduct to comply with the Twelfth Amendment, not to debase it through legerdemain [trickery]. Plaintiffs have thus failed to demonstrate a substantial likelihood of success on the merits of their claim that Secretary Cheney has been at some point since July 21, 2000, or will be on December 18, 2000, an inhabitant of the state of Texas.

The *Jones v. Bush* Decision Was Based on Broad Constitutional Interpretation

Jess Bravin

Jess Bravin is the Supreme Court correspondent for the Wall Street Journal. *In the following article, Bravin discusses the Twelfth Amendment and its habitation requirement for presidential and vice presidential candidates. This issue arose during the turmoil of the 2000 election when vice presidential candidate Dick Cheney's status as an inhabitant of Wyoming came under question. Bravin describes the details of the court case* Jones v. Bush *and shows how both sides attempted to use the Twelfth Amendment to their advantage.*

The section of the Constitution at issue is the relatively obscure 12th Amendment, overshadowed by its neighbor, the 13th, which abolished slavery after the Civil War. Ratified after the disputed 1800 election, the 12th lays out a number of regulations for the Electoral College. The rule in question says a state's delegation can't vote for presidential and vice presidential candidates who are both from electors' home state.

Role of the Twelfth Amendment in the 2000 Election

The 12th Amendment sat silently on the books for 196 years until the [George W.] Bush–[Dick] Cheney ticket, after falling 543,895 votes short of the [Al] Gore–[Joseph] Lieberman ticket, nevertheless stood poised to claim 271 electoral votes to the Democrats' 266.

Jess Bravin, "Obscure Texas Case Offers Peek into Role of Court Nominee," *The Wall Street Journal*, October 7, 2005. Republished with permission of The Wall Street Journal, conveyed through Copyright Clearance Center, Inc.

Annoyed by that prospect, three Texas voters filed suit under what they called the Constitution's Habitation Clause, seeking to prevent the state's 32 electoral votes from going to the Republicans. George W. Bush, then the state's governor, didn't deny his Texas standing, despite being born in Connecticut. But the plaintiffs also alleged that Mr. Cheney lived in Dallas as chief executive of Halliburton Co. Mr. Cheney contended he was a Wyomingite.

With *Bush v. Gore* heading to the U.S. Supreme Court, few took notice of *Jones v. Bush* when it was filed Nov. 20 in Dallas's federal courthouse. Mr. Bush understood the stakes and dispatched his crackerjack legal counselor Ms. [Harriet] Miers . . . [to handle the case.]

Texas or Wyoming?

According to court papers, Mr. Cheney bought a home and registered to vote in Dallas in 1995. After that date, he also held a Texas driver's license, paid Texas taxes and claimed the state's homestead tax deduction.

Mr. Cheney seemed aware of his Habitation Clause problem. In July 2000, shortly after deciding to run for vice president, he switched his voter registration and driver's license back to Wyoming. That detail formed part of his defense in the case, along with the fact that he had attended the University of Wyoming, represented Wyoming in Congress and owned a vacation home in Jackson Hole, Wyo.

Mr. Cheney also owned a Cadillac and a Lexus registered in Texas. He registered a Mercedes-Benz in Virginia, where he owned a townhouse, and a Jeep in Wyoming. The Miers team noted that Mr. Cheney put his Dallas home up for sale while the plaintiffs pointed out a listing describing it as "owner-occupied."

Ms. Miers's brief contended that for constitutional purposes, the relevant date was Dec. 18, 2000, the date the Elec-

Dick Cheney served as U.S. vice president from 2001 to 2009. © Matthew Cavanaugh/
hepa/Corbis.

toral College was scheduled to meet. By that time, Mr. Cheney
would have fully severed his Texas ties.

Noting that Mr. Cheney's wife Lynne had not switched her
voter registration to Wyoming from Texas, the plaintiffs pro-

posed to ask Mr. Cheney if he intended to live with his wife. "While I'm happy to say quite publicly that the marriage is good," said Mr. Cheney's lawyer David Aufhauser during a telephone conference, that question is "singularly offensive."

Mr. Aufhauser, Ms. Miers's co-counsel, suggested that whatever the 12th Amendment might have meant in 1804, the provision's meaning had, in effect, evolved with modern society. "Differences between the year 1800 and 2000 is more than two centuries, it's light years," said Mr. Aufhauser, noting the "rapidity with which each of us have changed addresses from schools and college to various marriages and jobs." ...

William Berenson, a Fort Worth lawyer representing the voter plaintiffs, insisted on a tighter interpretation of the clause, something more typical of the right. "I don't think that these Founding Fathers ... had in mind last-minute shenanigans where someone could start discarding baggage just at the last minute." The plaintiffs' brief noted that the Bush-Cheney ticket "promised to only appoint judges who would strictly interpret the Constitution."

Judge Fitzwater, a [President Ronald] Reagan appointee, sided with Ms. Miers's earlier argument that the plaintiffs lacked standing. On Dec. 1, he ruled that their "general interest in seeing that the government abides by the Constitution" fell short of the requirement that they have "an injury in fact to them personally."

He went [on] to opine that Mr. Cheney, for constitutional purposes, was a Wyomingite. "It is undisputed that he was born, raised, educated and married in Wyoming and represented the state as a member of Congress for six terms," Judge Fitzwater wrote, perhaps unaware that Mr. Cheney lists his birthplace as Lincoln, Neb. ...

Keith Whittington, author of "Constitutional Interpretation: Textual Meaning, Original Intent, and Judicial Review," notes that the Habitation Clause "is one of those provisions of the Constitution that just became irrelevant." The purpose was to prevent deadlock created by every delegation voting for its favorite son, he says. That problem disappeared as political parties became dominant.

Election Controversies in Contemporary America

The Electoral College Is a Misunderstood Institution

Danny M. Adkison and Christopher Elliott

Danny M. Adkison is an associate professor of political science at Oklahoma State University. Christopher Elliott attended the University of Mississippi School of Law. In the following essay, they argue that textbooks and teachers have been presenting incorrect facts regarding the electoral college and its operation. The authors suggest the idea that one needs to examine the actual Constitution to realize how the electoral college was intended to function. The problem as they see it is that too many authors or teachers use assumptions or false "common knowledge" about the electoral college without identifying what is actually in the founding document.

"It was of great importance not to make the government too complex." Thus did Caleb Strong, a Massachusetts delegate at the Constitutional Convention of 1787, argue against the use of the electoral college to select the president and vice president. Most college textbooks for the introductory American government course discuss the mechanics of the electoral college, so we decided to examine eighteen textbooks and their treatment of the electoral college. Written by prominent political scientists, these texts contain many errors on the workings of the electoral college. It would appear Strong's concern was a valid one.

Some might object to an examination of the accuracy with which political scientists treat the electoral college as either trivial or a "cheap shot." Yet we pay close attention to treatment of the electoral college because it is of interest to many

Danny M. Adkison and Christopher Elliott, "The Electoral College: A Misunderstood Institution," *PS: Political Science and Politics*, vol. 30, March 1997, pp. 77–80. Copyright © Cambridge University Press 1997. Reprinted with permission of Cambridge University Press and the authors.

students. One subject for which otherwise unenthusiastic students *do* show enthusiasm and interest is the electoral college. Often, questions on the subject come up very early in the course. In fact, the electoral college is one of the few subjects that bring questions from all over the classroom and even from students who seldom speak up. Authors of introductory American government texts should therefore be accurate in their description of the mechanics of the electoral college. Also, at least every four years the reform or abolishment of the electoral college is proposed. Yet, one cannot evaluate ideas for reform or abolition without accurate information on how the electoral college works.

Selection of Electors

One of the most common errors in the texts we examined relates to selection of electors. Here is what the Constitution stipulates: "Each State shall appoint, in such Manner as the Legislature thereof may direct, a Number of Electors, . . ." (Article II, Section I, Clause 2). Several selection methods were proposed at the Constitutional Convention: by state legislatures, by governors, and popular election. Convention delegates, probably motivated by the desire to secure ratification, left it to the states. Three basic methods of selection were used in the first presidential election: state legislature, popular vote, and a hybrid of these two methods. States experimented with various methods, ultimately settling on popular election, but are still constitutionally free to use their method of choice.

Several texts, however, imply that selection by state legislatures is the constitutionally mandated method. One text states, "they [the Framers] designed a selection system of 'electors' chosen by state legislatures." Four texts make this error. They state that the Framers assigned selection to the voters, and another stipulated that either the voters or the legislature could select the electors. Seven texts do not mention the constitu-

The president is officially elected by the officials within the Electoral College, and not the popular vote, which is cause for much debate. "To the Electoral College Again," cartoon by Bob Englehart. Copyright 2004 Bob Englehart and CagleCartoons.com. All rights reserved.

tional provision concerning the selection of electors, while three correctly report that each state can select the method for choosing electors.

Winner-Take-All

States also control the electoral college by how they allocate the vote. The Constitution does not prescribe a method. Tradition has resulted in all but two states using the winner-take-all system, sometimes known as the "general ticket system" or "unit rule." Under this system, the slate of electors (considered pledged to a particular candidate) with a plurality of the state-wide vote wins the right to cast the state's electoral votes.

It is important to note that unit rule is not constitutionally prescribed. It is a choice made by the states. One of the strongest criticisms of the electoral college is the possibility that the popular vote winner can be the electoral vote loser.

Unit rule is one reason for this possibility. Thus, students frequently characterize this system as unfair and cite it as a major reason for abolishing the electoral college. It is important, therefore, to note that unit rule was not mandated by the Framers, need not be amended out of the Constitution, but can, at any time, be changed by state law.

This distinction is frequently absent from the texts. It would be misleading for a text to imply that unit rule is *the* system for allocation of electoral votes. Yet, several texts do imply this by not mentioning that the Constitution does not *require* this system. For example, [George] McKenna reports, "the electoral college system awards all of the state's electoral votes to the candidate who wins a majority of popular votes in the state." Not only does the author attribute the winner-take-all method to the electoral college *system*, he also mistakenly reports it is based on a majority rather than a plurality vote. This is not the only text that mistakenly uses majority rather than plurality. In another example, the authors write, "The Constitution also created a system whereby the president is . . . chosen by an electoral college . . . this is a 'winner take all' method."

Some texts indirectly point out state choice by noting (often in a footnote) that Maine and Nebraska do not use the winner-take-all system. One text failed even to discuss how the votes are allocated; three texts do not mention the Maine and Nebraska exceptions; and four incorrectly report that Maine is the only state using a different system.

The Wrong Choice

The electoral college is probably most criticized for the possibility that the national popular vote winner can be the electoral vote loser. The general ticket system discussed above, which all but two states opt to use, contributes to this possibility. If one candidate wins landslides in popular votes in certain states (but not the requisite majority of electoral votes) and barely loses in the remaining states, the electoral winner can in fact be the popular vote loser. How many times has this happened?

Only in 1888 did a candidate win in the electoral college, yet lose in the national popular vote.[1] The textbooks, however, tell a different story. [William] Lasser writes, "It has actually happened twice in American history—in 1876 and 1888." But the electoral college did not decide the 1876 election, and neither was the House contingency used. That year, the Hayes-Tilden Commission decided disputed electoral votes and awarded them to Hayes, who received fewer popular votes than Tilden. Two other texts give two dates for the electoral college making the "wrong" choice. Of the twelve texts touching on this subject, five give three dates: 1824, 1876, and 1888. In 1824, the House contingency was used to elect John Quincy Adams in spite of the fact that Andrew Jackson had more popular votes.

The "wrong choice" phenomenon is typically used as a major reason for abolishing the electoral college. Textbook authors describe it as "distressing," "a serious objection," "the most serious criticism," "the most troubling aspect," and "undemocratic." When mentioning this phenomenon the texts typically lump the three elections (1824, 1876, and 1888) together. The authors usually fail to mention the role of the general ticket system (which is *not* required by the Constitution) in furthering the possibility, and they fail to distinguish the 1824 and 1876 elections which were not due to mathematical circumstances, but rather to the House contingency and Hayes-Tilden Commission respectively.

Other Errors

If textbook authors did not make an error concerning the above topics, they often made other errors or misleading state

1. Since this article was written (1997), another election was determined by the electoral vote going to the loser of the popular vote: *Bush v. Gore* in 2000.

ments. For instance, [one text] reports that the Framers wanted only male electors. Of course, that *may* be true, but when that statement is preceded by citation of Article II, Section 1, the reader might be led to believe this was constitutionally mandated.

One text incorrectly states that when the Senate contingency is used to elect the vice president "each state has one vote". In fact, the delegates debated this at the Convention and approved per capita voting.

Some texts, when discussing the House contingency, state that the Representatives must "choose from the five highest candidates." In fact, the Constitution did state this, though the 12th Amendment does require the contingency to choose from the top three candidates.

One text sustains the myth that the Constitution prohibits the election of a president and a vice president from the same state. Although the Constitution does prohibit an elector from casting both votes for candidates from the same state, this does not rule out the election of a president and vice president from the same state. Use of the contingency plans could also produce a president and vice president of the same state.

The Framers might be shocked to learn that the electoral tie between [Thomas] Jefferson and [Aaron] Burr was due to a "defect in the language of the Constitution." This would particularly surprise the Framers since they included a provision in the Constitution stating, "if there be more than one who have such Majority [of electoral votes], and have an equal Number of Votes, then the House of Representatives shall immediately" elect one of them president (Article II, Section 1, Clause 3, superseded by the 12th Amendment).

Another text errantly states that the 12th Amendment "was passed to prevent a president from being saddled with an opposing presidential candidate as vice-president." If that were true, it would probably have been proposed during the Federalist administration of [John] Adams when the Democratic-Republican Jefferson served as his vice president. The 12th Amendment was passed, rather, so that the electors could specify which vote was going for president and which for vice president.

Prior to the 12th Amendment, a presidential candidate elected vice president did not need a majority of the electors to win. The Framers, in their elaborate design, had a reason for this: the first vote cast by an elector would go to the state's favorite son, and thus the vice president would come from this list. Anticipating a dispersed vote, they did not require a majority vote. Hardly any of the authors described this detail, but [one text] contradicted the Framers' design by stating that under the original Constitution both president and vice president needed a majority of the electors to win.

In one text, the complexity of explaining the electoral college resulted in a gross historical error: "In 1796 . . . a tie in the electoral college sent the election into the House of Representatives, which selected Federalist John Adams as president and his political opponent, the Democratic-Republican Thomas Jefferson, as vice president." However, the presidential election of 1796 was *not* decided by the House of Representatives; Adams won a majority of the whole number of electors, while Jefferson came in second. . . .

Accuracy Is Important

Although errors can be found in any textbook, it is important for political scientists to correctly describe the electoral college. . . . When students raise questions about the electoral college, professors should be able to answer them without pointing out problems or errors in their textbooks.

The Electoral College Had Dubious Beginnings and Is No Longer Necessary

Akhil Reed Amar and Vikram David Amar

Brothers Akhil Reed Amar and Vikram David Amar both write about the law. Akhil teaches at Yale Law School and clerked for Justice Stephen Breyer before the latter's appointment to the U.S. Supreme Court. Vikram clerked for Judge William Norris and Justice Harry Blackmun and teaches at the University of California, Davis School of Law. They have individually or together published more than one hundred law review articles and several books. In the following article, they argue that the basis for the electoral college is sometimes taken for granted and that people do not perceive the effect the college has had on the U.S. political system. They argue that the electoral college and the Twelfth Amendment have had a large influence on race and sexual politics and have dramatically affected the elections for president.

On the first anniversary of the very odd election of 2000, it's hard to look back without fixating on Florida and the courts. But these absorbing soap operas should not obscure the other historical headline: the national popular vote loser nonetheless won the electoral college vote.

Is this a flaw in our Constitution? Should we scrap the electoral college in favor of direct popular vote? Practically speaking, can we do so? ...

Let's begin by considering why the Philadelphia Framers invented an intricate electoral college contraption in the first place, and why, after its gears jammed in the Adams-Jefferson-

Akhil Reed Amar and Vikram David Amar, "History, Slavery, Sexism, the South, and the Electoral College," *FindLaw.com*, November 20, 2001. Reproduced by permission. http://writ.news.findlaw.com/amar/20011130.html.

Burr election of 1800–01, the Twelfth Amendment repaired the thing rather than junking it. Why didn't early Americans simply opt for direct national election of the President? The typical answers taught in grade-school civics miss much of the real story, both by misreading the evidence from Philadelphia and ignoring the significance of later events, especially the Twelfth Amendment.

The Electoral College Does Not Really Help Small States—nor Was It Designed To

It's often said that the Founders chose the electoral college over direct election in order to balance the interests of big (high population) and small (low population) states. The key Philadelphia concession to small states was the Framers' back-up selection system: if no candidate emerged with a first-round electoral-vote majority, then the House of Representatives would choose among the top five finalists, with each state casting one vote, regardless of population. According to the standard story, although big states would predictably dominate the first round, small states could expect to loom large in the final selection.

But as James Madison insisted, the deepest political divisions in early America were not between big and small states as such; rather, the real fissures separated north from south, and east from west. Moreover, once the modern system of national presidential parties and winner-take-all state contests emerged—a system already visible, though not yet entrenched, at the time of the Twelfth Amendment—the big states obviously had the advantage.

With two national presidential parties, one candidate almost always had an electoral majority in the first round, rendering the Framers' pro-small-state back-up system irrelevant. (Three or four strong candidates, in contrast, might have split the vote so that no one garnered a majority.) And winner-

Brown University students protest the 2000 election results. AP Images.

take-all rules—under which a candidate who won a state got all of its electoral votes, not a number proportional to the extent of his win—compounded the advantage of big states.

Indeed, before the Civil War Amendments (which changed the electoral college yet again), only one of the sixteen presidents hailed from a small state—Franklin Pierce of New Hampshire. And of the twenty-six men to hold the office since the Civil War, only Bill Clinton of Arkansas claimed residence in a small state.

In sum, if the Framers' true goal was to give small states a leg up, they did a rather bad job of it. . . .

How the Founders' Concern About Voter Information Was Rendered Obsolete

Another Founding-era argument for the electoral college stemmed from the following objection to direct election: ordinary Americans across a vast continent would lack sufficient information to choose intelligently among leading presidential candidates.

This objection is sometimes described today as reflecting a general Founding distrust of democracy. But that is not quite right; after all, the Framers required that the House be directly elected every two years sharply breaking with the indirect election of Congressmen under the Articles of Confederation. Many leading Federalists also supported direct election of governors.

The key objection at Philadelphia was thus not to democracy per se, but to democracy based on inadequate voter information. The Founders believed that although voters in a given state would know enough to choose between leading state candidates for House races and for the governorship, these voters would likely lack information about which out-of-state figure would be best for the presidency.

This objection rang true in the 1780s, when life was far more local. But the early emergence of national presidential parties rendered the objection obsolete by linking presidential candidates to slates of local candidates and national platforms that explained to voters who stood for what. . . .

The Key Role of Slavery in the History of the Electoral College

The biggest flaw in standard civics accounts of the electoral college is that they never mention the real demon dooming direct national election in 1787 and 1803: slavery.

At the Philadelphia convention, the visionary Pennsylvanian James Wilson proposed direct national election of the President. But in a key speech on July 19, the savvy Virginian James Madison suggested that such a system would prove unacceptable to the South: "The right of suffrage was much more diffusive in the Northern than the Southern States; and the latter could have no influence in the election on the score of Negroes."

In other words, in a direct election system, the North would outnumber the South, whose many slaves (more than half a million in all) of course could not vote. But the electoral college—a prototype of which Madison proposed in this same speech—instead let each southern state count its slaves, albeit with a two-fifths discount, in computing its share of the overall electoral college.

Virginia emerged as the big winner—the California of the Founding era—with 12 out of a total of 91 electoral votes allocated by the Philadelphia Constitution, more than a quarter of the 46 needed to win in the first round. After the 1800 census, Wilson's free state of Pennsylvania had ten percent more free persons than Virginia, but got twenty percent fewer electoral votes. Perversely, the more slaves Virginia (or any other slave state) bought or bred, the more electoral votes it would receive. Were a slave state to free any blacks who then moved North, the state could actually lose electoral votes.

If the system's pro-slavery tilt was not overwhelmingly obvious when the Constitution was ratified, it quickly became so. For 32 of the Constitution's first 36 years, a white slaveholding Virginian occupied the Presidency.

Southerner Thomas Jefferson, for example, won the election of 1800–01 against Northerner John Adams in a race where the slavery-skew of the electoral college was the decisive margin of victory: without the extra electoral college votes generated by slavery, the mostly southern states that supported Jefferson would not have sufficed to give him a majority. As pointed observers remarked at the time, Thomas Jefferson metaphorically rode into the executive mansion on the backs of slaves.

The 1796 contest between Adams and Jefferson had featured an even sharper division between northern states and southern states. Thus, when the Twelfth Amendment tinkered with the electoral college system rather than tossing it, the system's pro-slavery bias was hardly a secret.

Indeed, in the floor debate over the amendment in late 1803, Massachusetts Congressman Samuel Thatcher complained that "The representation of slaves adds thirteen members to this House in the present Congress, and eighteen Electors of President and Vice President at the next election." But Thatcher's complaint went unredressed. Once again, the North caved to the South by refusing to insist on direct national election.

How the Electoral College Hurt Women's Suffrage as Well

The Founding fathers' electoral college also didn't do much for the Founding mothers.

In a system of direct national election, any state that chose to enfranchise its women would have automatically doubled its clout in presidential elections. (New Jersey apparently did allow some women to vote in the Founding era, but later abandoned the practice.)

Under the electoral college, however, a state had no special incentive to expand suffrage—each state got a fixed number of electoral votes based on population, regardless of how many or how few citizens were allowed to vote or actually voted. As with slaves, what mattered was simply how many women resided in a state, not how many could vote there.

In light of this more complete (if less flattering) account of the electoral college in the late eighteenth and early nineteenth century, Americans must ask themselves whether we want to maintain this peculiar institution in the twenty-first century.

After all, most millennial Americans no longer believe in slavery or sexism. We do not believe that voters lack proper information about national candidates. We do not believe that a national figure claiming a national mandate is unacceptably dangerous. What we do believe is that each American is an equal citizen. We celebrate the idea of one person, one voter—an idea undermined by the electoral college.

The Effects of the Electoral College on the 2000 Presidential Election

Kenneth Jost and Greg Giroux

Kenneth Jost, Supreme Court editor for CQ Press and associate editor of CQ Researcher, *is a professor at Georgetown University School of Law and the editor of* The Supreme Court, A to Z. *Greg Giroux is a senior reporter for* Congressional Quarterly *who specializes in politics and elections. In the following viewpoint, Jost and Giroux give an overview of the electoral battle that occurred after the 2000 election. The authors discuss the electoral college's role in the situation and point out that this has led some to call for the abolishing of the system.*

The 2000 presidential race produced one of the closest popular-vote margins in U.S. history and left neither Republican George W. Bush nor Democrat Al Gore with an Electoral College majority on the day after the election. . . .

Florida's 25 electoral votes emerged as the critical prize in the 2000 presidential race in the early morning hours of Nov. 8, as the popular-vote totals from the other 49 states and the District of Columbia left neither Bush nor Gore with a majority of the nation's 538 electoral votes. But the popular vote in Florida was close—so close that four weeks later both Bush and Gore [were] claiming victory.

The tortuously close vote in the contest to elect the nation's 43rd president [gave] Americans a crash course in the little-understood mechanics of the 212-year-old Electoral College voting system. Americans accustomed to thinking that they were directly voting for president and vice president now

Kenneth Jost and Greg Giroux, "Electoral College: Should It Be Abolished? Should It Be Changed?" *CQ Researcher Online*, December 8, 2000. Copyright © 2008 CQ Press, a Division of Sage Publications. Reproduced by permission.

know that they are really voting for a number of electors from their state equal to the size of the state's congressional delegation: two senators plus the number of representatives, which is determined by the state's population.

In addition, Americans [have learned] that the presidential election is not over the morning after Election Day but continues through myriad other steps, including formal certification of the states' popular votes; meetings of the states' electors in their respective state capitals in mid-December; and the formal counting of electoral votes by a joint session of Congress in early January, two weeks before inauguration on Jan. 20.

The Electoral College has been controversial throughout U.S. history. More than 700 proposals to change it have been introduced in Congress over the past 200 years. Critics—many who favor direct election—call the college anachronistic and anti-democratic. . . .

Supporters, however, view the Electoral College as a bulwark of federalism and the two-party system. In any event, the supporters say, it works—most of the time without a hitch. . . .

Electoral Cliffhanger

Al Gore and George W. Bush wrapped up their parties' nominations for the presidency early in the 2000 campaign and swapped leads in public-opinion polls at the end of the parties' respective national conventions. Political observers of all persuasions were forecasting one of the closest presidential contests in history. Then, as Election Day neared, experts and strategists were openly speculating that one candidate might win the popular-vote contest only to lose the presidency on electoral votes.

In the most common scenario, observers speculated that Bush—who led in the polls in the week before the election—could lead the popular vote while Gore won an Electoral Col-

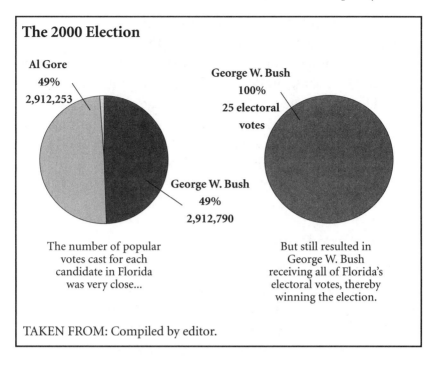

The 2000 Election

Al Gore
49%
2,912,253

George W. Bush
100%
25 electoral
votes

George W. Bush
49%
2,912,790

The number of popular votes cast for each candidate in Florida was very close...

But still resulted in George W. Bush receiving all of Florida's electoral votes, thereby winning the election.

TAKEN FROM: Compiled by editor.

lege majority by capturing most of the country's biggest states, including California and New York, where he held commanding leads. Less frequently, observers speculated that Gore might win the popular-vote tally while Bush claimed the electoral vote by sweeping the Sun Belt and Mountain states, including the third and fourth biggest prizes: Texas and Florida. . . .

On the eve of the election, officials in both campaigns were predicting complete victories for their candidates. Karl Rove, Bush's chief strategist, was forecasting a six- or seven-point margin in the popular vote and "a substantial margin" of around 320 electoral votes. Gore campaign Chairman William Daley predicted a two-and-a-half to three-point margin and 290 electoral votes.

The actual election results confounded the experts: Gore held a popular-vote lead of about 200,000 votes the day after the election, while the electoral vote outcome hung on the close contest in Florida. On Nov. 8, as Florida began a mandatory recount under state law, Gore acknowledged that his popular-vote victory was not determinative.

"Despite the fact that Joe Lieberman and I won the popular vote," Gore said, "under our Constitution, it is the winner of the Electoral College who will be the next president."

For his part, Bush expressed confidence in an ultimate victory. "It's going to be resolved quickly," he said of the Florida recount. Then, with running mate [Dick] Cheney at his side, Bush declared: "I'm confident that the secretary and I will be president-elect and vice president-elect." . . .

Recounts and Contests

Nearly three weeks after 6 million Floridians cast their ballots in the presidential election, the state's three-member canvassing board announced the "certified" results in a nationally televised, early Sunday evening session on Nov. 26. The count gave Bush a 537-vote victory over Gore: 2,912,790 to 2,912,253.

"Accordingly, on behalf of the State Elections Canvassing Commission and in accordance with the laws of the State of Florida," Secretary of State [Katherine] Harris concluded, "I hereby declare Gov. George W. Bush the winner of Florida's 25 electoral votes for the president of the United States." . . .

Harris' announcement of a normally routine post-election procedure followed an extraordinary political and legal drama that included contentious and excruciatingly tedious manual recounts of votes in several of Florida's 67 counties and lawsuits that traversed state and federal courts up to the U.S. Supreme Court. And far from concluding the election, the announcement only set the stage for an unprecedented election contest by Gore in Florida courts challenging the officially certified results as inaccurate. . . .

The unofficial Bush lead of 1,784 votes in Florida triggered a state law requiring an automatic recount whenever the margin in a race is less than one-half of 1 percent of the votes cast. Over the next four days, most counties in the state completed machine recounts—and Bush's margin fell to 327 votes. Meanwhile, the Gore campaign had asked for hand recounts in four heavily Democratic counties: Volusia, along the central East Coast, and Broward, Palm Beach and Dade in South Florida. . . .

The major legal dispute, though, turned on the deadline for counties to submit election returns to Harris' office. In one longstanding section, Florida law provided that any returns not submitted by 5 p.m. of the seventh day after the election "shall be ignored."

Another section added in 1989, however, provided that returns received after the deadline "may be ignored." With manual recounts incomplete in the three South Florida counties, the apparent conflict between the two sections left unclear whether the amended totals could be included in the final returns. Harris said she would enforce the deadline and ignore late-filed recounts—triggering accusations of partisanship from the Gore campaign and a suit by the Volusia County election board, later joined by the Palm Beach board, seeking to force her to accept the recounts when finished.

Leon County Circuit Judge Terry Lewis gave the Gore campaign an initial boost on Nov. 14 by ruling that Harris had to exercise discretion in determining whether to accept or reject late-filed returns. The next day, Harris reaffirmed her original position, saying the discretion for late filings was intended only in cases of mechanical breakdowns or natural disasters.

After a second round of arguments—this time by lawyers for Gore and the Florida Democratic Party—Lewis ruled on Nov. 17 that Harris had adequately complied with his previous order and upheld her decision to reject the recounts.

The ruling seemed to be a fatal setback for Gore, but the Florida Supreme Court promptly stepped in by agreeing to hear the case and barring Harris from certifying election results in the meantime. The seven justices—six of them appointed by Democratic governors and a seventh jointly appointed in 1998 by outgoing Democrat Lawton Chiles and then Gov.-elect Jeb Bush—heard more than two hours of arguments from a battery of lawyers in a nationally televised court session on Nov. 20. Late the next evening, the court issued a unanimous, 42-page decision requiring Harris to include the late-filed returns before certifying the results.

"An accurate vote count is one of the essential foundations of our democracy," the court declared. The right to vote, the justices said, took precedence over what they called "a hyper-technical reliance" upon the seven-day deadline provision. With no other deadline set in the law, the court itself created one. It said Harris must include any returns submitted by 5 p.m., Sunday, Nov. 26—or by 9 a.m., Monday, Nov. 27, if her office was not open on Sunday. . . .

The state high court ruling touched off a frenzy of activity as the Thanksgiving holiday weekend approached. Election workers in Broward, Dade and Palm Beach counties worked in round-the-clock shifts, peering at punch-card ballots to try to discern voters' intentions from chads that were either partially detached ("hanging") or indented ("dimpled" or "pregnant"). Bush's lawyers insisted the process was inherently subjective. But Democrats defended the procedure, saying that it complied with Florida law—and with a Texas statute that Bush himself had signed. . . .

Meanwhile, Bush had taken the deadline extension issue to the U.S. Supreme Court. His lawyers contended that the state high court had violated federal law and the U.S. Constitution by changing the election rules after the balloting. Defying virtually unanimous predictions from legal experts, the Supreme Court agreed on Nov. 24 to hear the case and scheduled oral arguments for Dec. 1.

As the Thanksgiving weekend came to a close, Gore supporters acknowledged that the recounts were not going to yield enough votes to reverse Bush's apparent lead. Even before the official certification, Gore himself signaled his intention to file an election challenge in a lunchtime interview with the *New York Times* that was posted on the newspaper's Web site by mid-afternoon.

Bush, however, was undeterred. Two hours after Harris' announcement, the Texas governor stood in the Texas state capitol to claim victory and to urge Gore to drop plans to contest the election further. "Now that the votes are counted," Bush said, "it is time for the votes to count." . . .

At the Supreme Court, the justices appeared divided during an extended, 90-minute argument Dec. 1 in Bush's appeal of the Florida Supreme Court decision extending the certification deadline. Three days later, though, the court issued a unanimous decision that dealt Gore a setback. The justices set aside the Florida high court's decision, saying there was "considerable uncertainty" about the basis for the ruling.

Legally, the unsigned ruling was murky, though it indicated sympathy for Bush's position. In any event, the ruling erased the Florida high court's decision for the moment, restored Bush's 930-vote margin, and denied Gore the kind of legal and public relations victory needed to press his bid for a recount. . . .

The fierce legal battle for Florida's 25 electoral votes—and the presidency—has inevitably evoked comparisons to the Electoral College's darkest moment: the Tilden-Hayes race of 1876, decided by an ostensibly bipartisan commission that divided strictly along partisan lines. For the most part, though, politicians, advocates and observers were insisting that the recount battle did not amount to a constitutional crisis. "Our Constitution can handle a lot," Jonathan Turley, a law professor at George Washington University in Washington, remarked.

Experts are divided on the question whether the Electoral College system has exacerbated the difficulties of the Florida recount. Supporters of direct election say the fight for Florida's electoral votes would have been less important—and therefore perhaps not fought at all—if the race simply went to the popular-vote winner. Supporters of the Electoral College counter that direct election would actually increase the risk of nasty vote recounts anywhere in the country as well as the danger of partisan manipulation of voting procedures by dominant parties in each state. . . .

The uncertainty over the outcome in Florida also highlighted the pitfalls of the Electoral College system's existing procedures for resolving deadlocks. Most observers seemed apprehensive at best about the possibility of throwing the election into the House of Representatives, having Congress decide on the validity of electoral votes, or allowing the Florida legislature to select the state's presidential electors. "Ticking time bombs," Yale law Professor [Akhil Reed] Amar called those options.

Some supporters of the Electoral College say they do favor some changes in the system—such as shifting to district-by-district awarding of electoral votes or making the electoral votes automatic to eliminate the problem [of] "faithless electors." But they warn that broader changes would lead to unforeseeable consequences. "If we change this, everything will change," [professor Judith] Best says. . . .

For their part, opponents of the Electoral College concede that efforts to change or abolish the system face long odds but insist the 2000 presidential race proves the need for change. "It probably won't happen, but we're going to have to generate a debate on it," Georgetown's [Stephen] Wayne says. "It's going to take time, but to me no purpose is served by the person with the most votes not winning."

"There have been a few glitches, but there would have been glitches with any system," [professor Michael] Glennon responds. "As James Madison said, there was no system they looked at that had no flaws. They picked the least imperfect system."

States Move to Change the Electoral College

Jennifer Steinhauer

Jennifer Steinhauer is a writer for the New York Times. *In the following viewpoint, she examines how some states have become dissatisfied with the current method of electing the president via the electoral college. These states have proposed altering the way presidents are elected by switching the system over to a direct popular voting or voting via congressional district system. States as large as California to smaller states like Maryland have begun a movement to alter the election system.*

Frustrated by a system that has marginalized many states in the presidential election process, or seeking partisan advantage, state lawmakers, political party leaders and voting rights advocates across the country are stepping up efforts to change the rules of the game, even as the [2008] presidential campaign advances.

States Seek Alternatives to the Electoral College

In California, this has led to a nascent Republican bid to apportion the state's electoral votes by Congressional district, not by statewide vote, in a move that most everyone agrees would benefit Republican candidates. Democrats in North Carolina are mulling a similar move, because it would help Democrats there. . . .

Further, there is a germinal movement to effectively abolish the Electoral College, awarding the White House instead to the winner of the national popular vote. Maryland recently

Jennifer Steinhauer, "Frustrated, States Try to Change the Way Presidents Are Elected," *New York Times*, August 11, 2007, p. A1. Copyright © 2007 by The New York Times Company. Reproduced by permission.

became the first state to have such legislation passed and then signed into law, although legislatures in several other states have passed similar measures.

"There are different political fires all over the place," Mr. [Art] Torres [the California Democratic Party chairman] said. "We felt before that we would try and maintain some order and discipline, but it has been difficult to do. This all portends a strong initiative by states to exert more power."

Each maneuver, which experts on electoral politics agree could radically change the political landscape or, just as easily, completely wash out, has added a generous dose of unpredictability to an already knotty federal election season. . . .

The states' efforts reflect a momentum outside Washington to "get a system that reflects public preferences," said George C. Edwards III, a professor of political science at Texas A&M University. Elected officials, state party leaders and many voters have grown weary of a system in which "candidates focus on 13 or 14 states and no other states get attention, except for fund-raising," Professor Edwards said.

In 2004, 13 states with 159 electoral votes among them were considered "in play," according to FairVote, a voting rights organization; in 1988, there were 21 such states and 272 electoral votes.

The interest in changing the way the president is elected was largely seeded by Democrats after the 2000 election, but has since been embraced by Republicans as well.

"We have discovered what our founding fathers learned as well, which is that you can manipulate election outcomes by setting those rules," said Michael P. McDonald, an associate professor of government and politics at George Mason University.

In the [spring 2007] legislative session, lawmakers in eight states considered bills that would give their electoral votes to the winner of the national popular vote rather than the presidential candidate chosen by state voters; the measures would

North Dakota legislator Duane DeKrey sponsored a bill in 2007 that proposed to elect future presidents by popular vote instead of the electoral college system. AP Images.

take effect only if states representing a majority of the 538 electoral votes made the same change.

"The idea of the states banding together and being able to set the rules of the game to directly elect the president is a new idea," said Pete Maysmith, the national director of state campaigns for Common Cause, which advocates a national popular vote. "And I think it is grabbing people's attention and gaining momentum."

Far more potentially significant in the near term, however, is a recent move by the lawyer for the California Republican Party to ask voters in a ballot measure to apportion electoral votes by Congressional district. With numerous safe Republican districts around the state, this change could represent roughly 20 electoral votes for a Republican candidate who would otherwise presumably lose the entire state, which has been reliably Democrat in recent presidential elections.

"We think it is the most effective way of having California count," said Kevin Eckery, a spokesman for the ballot effort, the Presidential Election Reform Act. "Candidates love California in the spring when they come out to raise money. But after that, as long as California is not in play, it tends to be ignored." . . .

While assigning electoral votes by Congressional district is a movement lacking broad national support, both Republicans and Democrats agreed that should the effort by California Republicans gain steam, other states might consider it as well, if for no other reason than to counter the anticipated Republican gains [t]here. Only Maine and Nebraska currently use such a system.

Had the electoral votes been allocated by Congressional district nationwide in 2000, President [George W.] Bush's electoral margin of victory would have been just over 7 percent, or eight times his take that year, according to FairVote.

The Electoral College Does Not Result in an Equality of Votes

George C. Edwards III

George C. Edwards III, Distinguished Professor of Political Science and the George and Julia Blucher Jordan Chair in Presidential Studies in the Bush School of Government and Public Service at Texas A&M University, is editor of Presidential Studies Quarterly *and the author of numerous books. He argues in the following viewpoint that the electoral college, as an indirect method of electing the president, does not allow for equality of vote counting. Edwards points out that political equality is key in a democracy and that this system is diminishing popular votes by translating them into electoral votes.*

The electoral college does not provide a straightforward process for selecting the president. Instead, it can be extraordinarily complex and has the potential to undo the people's will at many points in the long journey from the selection of electors to counting their votes in Congress. Faithless electors may fail to vote as the people who elected them wish. Congress may find it difficult to choose justly between competing slates of electors. It is even possible, although highly unlikely, that a state legislature could take the choice of the electors away from the people altogether. The electoral college poses an even more fundamental threat to American democracy, however.

Political Equality

Political equality lies at the core of democratic theory. Robert Dahl, the leading democratic theorist, includes equality in vot-

George C. Edwards III, *Why the Electoral College Is Bad for America*, New Haven, CT: Yale University Press, 2004. Copyright © 2004 by Yale University. All rights reserved. Reproduced by permission.

ing as a central standard for a democratic process: "every member must have an equal and effective opportunity to vote, and all votes must be counted as equal." A constitution for democratic government, he adds, "must be in conformity with one elementary principle: that all members are to be treated (under the Constitution) as if they were equally qualified to participate in the process of making decisions about the policies the association will pursue. Whatever may be the case on other matters, then, in governing this association all members are to be considered as *politically equal*." . . .

Even those who gave us the Constitution came to have doubts about its violations of political equality. James Madison, the most influential of all the delegates to the Constitutional Convention, was writing as early as 1792 in the *National Gazette* about the importance of "establishing political equality among all" and arguing that no group should have influence out of proportion to its numbers. Forty-one years later, he was still at it, writing in 1833 that republican government is the "least imperfect" form of government and "the vital principle of republican government is . . . the will of the majority." . . .

The Translation of Popular Votes into Electoral Votes

A popular misconception is that electoral votes are simple aggregates of popular votes. In reality, the electoral vote regularly deviates from the popular will as expressed in the popular vote—sometimes merely in curious ways, usually strengthening the electoral edge of the popular vote leader, but at times in such a way as to deny the presidency to the popular preference. Popular votes do not equal electoral votes—the former express the people's choice, while the latter determine who is to be the people's president. . . .

The Winner-Take-All (Unit-Vote) System

The operation of the winner-take-all system effectively disenfranchises voters who support losing candidates in each state. In the 2000 presidential election, nearly three million people voted for Al Gore for president in Florida. Because George W. Bush won 537 more votes than Gore, however, he received *all* of Florida's electoral votes. . . .

A candidate thus can win some states by very narrow margins, lose other states by large margins (as Bush did in California and New York in 2000), and so win the electoral vote while losing the popular vote. The votes for candidates who do not finish first in a state play no role in the outcome of the election, since they are not aggregated across states.

For every other office in the country—every governor, every legislator, on both the state and the national level—we aggregate the votes for the candidates across the entire constituency of the office. Only for the presidency do we fail to count the votes for the candidate who does not win a subsection of the constituency. The winner-take-all system takes the electoral votes allocated to a state based on its population and awards them all to the plurality winner of the state. *In effect, the system gives the votes of the people who voted against the winner to the winner.*

In a multiple-candidate contest (as in 1992, 1996, and 2000), the winner-take-all system may suppress the votes of the *majority* as well as the minority. In the presidential election of 1996, less than a majority of votes decided the blocs of electoral votes of twenty-six states. In 2000, pluralities rather than majorities determined the allocation of electoral votes in eight states, including Florida and Ohio. In each case, a minority of voters determined how *all* of their state's electoral votes would be cast.

In the three-candidate contest of 1992, 2,072,698, or 39 percent, of Florida's voters cast their ballots for Bill Clinton, and another 1,053,067 state voters, or 19.8 percent, chose Ross Perot, but Florida's twenty-five electoral-vote slate went as a bloc to George Bush on the basis of his popular vote plurality of 2,173,310, just 40.9 percent of the state vote. Nearly 59 percent of Florida's voters, 3,125,765 citizens, preferred Clinton or Perot but received no electoral votes reflecting their preferences. Arizona's electoral votes went to Bush on the basis of his state popular vote of only [about] 38.5 percent[, although some 61.5 percent] of the voters in that state supported other candidates. Conversely, in California in 1992, Bush won 3,630,574 votes, or 32.6 percent of the state total, and Perot 2,296,006, or 20.6 percent. Nevertheless, Clinton, with 46 percent of the state popular vote, received 100 percent of the state's fifty-four electoral votes. . . .

The winner-take-all system not only disenfranchises millions of Americans (distorting majority rule in the process, as we will see), it also distributes influence in selecting the president unequally. Large states enjoy a theoretical advantage in being more likely than small states to cast the pivotal bloc of electoral votes in the electoral college, and thus a citizen of a large state is hypothetically more likely to be able to cast the vote that will determine how his or her state's electoral votes will be cast. As [political scientists] George Rabinowitz and Elaine MacDonald have concluded, "In presidential elections, some citizens, by virtue of their physical location in a given state, are in a far better position to determine presidential outcomes than others . . . extreme inequities exist between the power of citizens living in different states." . . .

The Allocation of Electoral Votes Among States

The Constitution allocates electoral votes to each state equal to that state's representation in Congress. This system of distribution further diminishes the impact of the popular vote in electing the president in two ways. First, the number of House seats does not exactly match the population of a state. The populations of some states barely exceed the threshold for an additional seat while those in other states just miss it. ... The census figures used to determine the number of seats a state has in the House (and thus the electoral votes that match them) may be out of date. The allocation of electoral votes in the election of 2000 actually reflected the population distribution among the states of 1990, a decade earlier.

Depending on how one views the appropriate representation of noncitizens, the fact that many noncitizens reside in some states may be another distorting factor in the allocation of electoral votes. Representation in the House is based on the decennial census, which counts all residents—whether citizens or not. Such states as California, Florida, and New York, where noncitizens compose a substantial percentage of the population, receive more electoral votes than they would if electoral votes were allocated on the basis of the number of a state's citizens.

In addition, each state receives two electoral votes corresponding to the number of its U.S. senators. When states with unequal populations receive similar numbers of electoral votes, states with smaller populations gain a mathematical advantage.

Thus, every voter's ballot does not carry the same weight. That is, the ratio of electoral votes to population varies from state to state, benefiting the smallest states. In the most extreme case, for example, as of 2003, an electoral vote in Wyoming corresponded to only 167,081 persons, while one in California corresponded to 645,172 persons. The typical citizen of Wyoming, then, has on average four times as much influence in determining an electoral vote for president as the typical citizen of California. ...

Differences in Voter Turnout

There are substantial differences among states in the rate at which their citizens turn out to vote. For example, in 2000, only 44 percent of the voting age population of U.S. citizens in Hawaii, 46 percent in Georgia and West Virginia, and 47 percent in South Carolina and Texas voted in the presidential election. On the other hand, 71 percent of those in Minnesota, 69 percent of those in Maine and Alaska, and 68 percent of those in Wisconsin voted. These states had turnout rates about 50 percent greater than those states with low turnout.

In an election featuring voter equality, the number of potential voters who actually cast a vote matters, because votes are aggregated across the electorate and all votes count equally. In the electoral college, however, it does not matter whether one person or all eligible persons go to the polls. Because each state has a predetermined number of electoral votes, the actual vote total in a state has no relevance to its electoral votes. The state casts its electoral votes even if only one person actually votes.

As a result of differences in voter turnout, citizens who vote in states with high voter turnout have less influence on the selection of the president than citizens who vote in states with low turnout. For example, in 2000 in Minnesota, there was a ratio of about 243,000 voters per electoral vote. In Hawaii, by contrast, the ratio was only about 92,000 voters per electoral vote. Each Hawaiian who voted exercised 2.6 times as much influence on an electoral vote as each voting Minnesotan. . . .

Disparities Between Popular and Electoral Votes

One net result of these distorting factors is that there is typically a substantial disparity in almost all elections between the national popular vote a candidate receives and that candidate's percentage of the electoral vote.

In the election of 1860, although Stephen A. Douglas was second in popular votes, he was fourth in the electoral college. Although he won 74 percent as many popular votes as were cast for Abraham Lincoln, his electoral vote was just 6.7 percent of Lincoln's. Douglas's popular vote was 162 percent of John C. Breckinridge's, yet he received only 16.7 percent as many electoral votes as Breckinridge. And Douglas's popular vote exceeded John Bell's by more than two times, but Bell had three times as many votes in the electoral college. . . .

Noteworthy differences between popular and electoral votes also marked the three-way contest among Bill Clinton, George Bush, and Ross Perot in 1992. Winner Clinton received his solid 68.8 percent of the total electoral votes on the basis of a strikingly low 43 percent of the national popular vote, while Bush enjoyed no such electoral college bonus: his 37.4 percent of the popular votes was diminished by the electoral system to 31.2 percent of the electoral votes. This diminution was minor, however, in contrast to the electoral annihilation suffered by independent candidate Perot. In his personally financed, quixotic campaign, Perot won nearly 19 percent of the national vote. Despite winning more than nineteen million popular votes—the greatest number polled by any third-party candidate in the history of the Republic—Perot received precisely zero electoral votes. For Clinton, the electoral magnification of electoral votes over popular votes was 26 percentage points. . . .

The lack of close association between the winner's percentage of the popular vote and his percentage of the electoral vote is typical. There have been forty-four presidential elections since 1824. In only eight (18 percent) has the disparity between the winning candidate's popular and electoral vote been fewer than 10 percentage points. In twenty-one of these elections (48 percent), the disparities have exceeded 20 percentage points. . . .

Choice Must Belong to the People

Democratic elections do not always guarantee that the best candidate will win. But even when we admit that the vox populi ["voice of the people"] may err, the fact remains that through our entire national experience we have learned that there is no safer, no better way to elect our public officials than by the choice of the people, with the candidate who wins the most votes being awarded the office. This is the essence of "the consent of the governed." And no matter how wisely or foolishly the American people choose their president, their choice is *their* president. The choice of the chief executive must be the people's, and it should rest with none other than them.

The Electoral College Is a Necessary System and Remains Relevant

Michael M. Uhlmann

Michael M. Uhlmann teaches politics and constitutional law in the School of Politics and Economics at Claremont Graduate University in California. He has written articles and reviews for the Los Angeles Times, *the* National Review, *the* American Spectator, *the* Washington Times, First Things, Crisis, *and* Human Life Review. *In the following article Uhlmann argues that the Founding Fathers originally set up the electoral college system to ensure that there would not be a tyrannical majority—it was to defuse and moderate the will and wishes of the people. Uhlmann argues that the electoral college should be kept in place and that changing the way presidents are elected would alter the presidency itself.*

As the late [comedian] Rodney Dangerfield might say, the Electoral College just don't get no respect. Polls show that most Americans, given the opportunity, would cashier it tomorrow in favor of so-called direct election. That they'd live to regret their decision only reminds us of H.L. Mencken's definition of democracy: a form of government in which the people know what they want, and deserve to get it good and hard. What the people would get by choosing direct election is the disintegration of the state-based two-party system; the rise of numerous factional parties based on region, class, ideology, or cult of personality; radicalized public opinion, frequent runoff elections, widespread electoral fraud, and centralized control of the electoral process; and, ultimately, unstable national government that veers between incompetence and tyrannical caprice. And that's only a partial list.

Michael M. Uhlmann, "The Old (Electoral) College Cheer: Why We Have It; Why We Need It," *National Review*, November 8, 2004. Reproduced by permission.

Dissatisfaction with the electoral-vote system has been a staple of populist rhetoric ever since presidential elections became fully democratized in the 1820s. More than 700 constitutional amendments have been introduced to change the system—by far the greatest number on any subject—and although reform prescriptions have varied greatly in detail, their common assumption has always been that our electoral rules prevent the true voice of the people from being heard.

Majorities Can Be Tyrannical

But what is the "true voice" of the people? Public sentiment can be expressed and measured in any number of ways, but not all are conducive to securing rights. If ascertaining the consent of the people were only a matter of counting heads until you got to 50 percent plus one, we could dispense with most of the distinctive features of the Constitution—not only electoral votes, but also federalism, the separation of powers, bicameralism, and staggered elections. All of these devices depart from simple majoritarianism, and for good reason: Men do not suddenly become angels when they acquire the right to vote; an electoral majority can be just as tyrannical as autocratic kings or corrupt oligarchs.

The Founders believed that while the selfish proclivities of human nature could not be eliminated, their baleful effects could be mitigated by a properly designed constitutional structure. Although the Constitution recognizes no other source of authority than the people, it takes pains to shape and channel popular consent in very particular ways. Thomas Jefferson perfectly captured the Framers' intent in his First Inaugural Address: "All, too, will bear in mind this sacred principle, that though the will of the majority is in all cases to prevail, that will to be rightful must be reasonable; that the minority possess their equal rights, which equal law must protect, and to violate which would be oppression." By reasonable majorities, Jefferson meant those that would reflect popular sentiment but, by the very manner of their composition, would be unable or unlikely to suppress the rights and interests of those in the minority. Accordingly, the Constitution understands elections not as ends in themselves, but as a means of securing limited government and equal rights for all.

The presidential election system helps to form reasonable majorities through the interaction of its three distinguishing attributes: the distribution and apportionment of electoral votes in accordance with the federal principle; the requirement that the winner garner a majority of electoral votes; and the custom (followed by 48 of 50 states) of awarding all of a state's electoral votes to the popular-vote victor within that state. Working together, these features link the presidency to the federal system, discourage third parties, and induce moderation on the part of candidates and interest groups alike. No candidate can win without a broad national coalition, assembled state by state yet compelled to transcend narrow geographic, economic, and social interests.

Problems with Changing the Current System

Reformers tend to assume that the mode of the presidential election can be changed without affecting anything else. Not so. As Sen. John F. Kennedy argued in the 1950s, by changing the method of the presidential election, you change not only the presidency but the entire political solar system of which it is an integral part. The presidency is at once the apex of our constitutional structure and the grand prize of the party system. Our method of selecting a president is the linchpin that holds both together. Capturing the presidency is the principal *raison d'etre* of our political parties, whose structure, thanks to the electoral-vote system, mirrors the uniquely federal structure of the Constitution. This means that two-party competition is the norm; in a country of America's size and diversity, that is no small virtue.

With (for the most part) only two parties in contention, the major candidates are forced to appeal to most of the same voters. This drives them both toward the center, moderates their campaign rhetoric, and helps the winner to govern more effectively once in office. Many factional interests, for their part, are under a reciprocal inducement to buy insurance with both sides, meaning the compromises necessary for successful rule will be made prior to and not after the election. Moreover, by making the states the principal electoral battlegrounds, the current system tends to insulate the nation against the effects of local voting fraud. All in all, the current system forces the ambitions of presidential candidates into the same constitutional mold that defines and tempers American political life as a whole. It thereby prevents the presidency from becoming a potentially dangerous tutelary force separate and apart from the rest of the Constitution's structure. . . .

Proponents of direct election indict those delicate balances for being "undemocratic." That is true only in the most superficial sense. If the Electoral College is undemocratic, so are federalism, the United States Senate, and the procedure for constitutional amendment. So is bicameralism and, for that matter, the separation of powers, which among other things authorizes an unelected judiciary. These constitutional devices were once widely understood to be the very heart and soul of the effort to form reasonable majorities. If all you care about is the achievement of mathematical equality in presidential elections, and if to achieve that goal you're willing to eliminate the states' role in presidential elections, what other "undemocratic" features of the Constitution are you also willing to destroy? And when you're done hacking your way through the Constitution, what guarantee can you give that your mathematically equal majorities can be restrained? How will you constrain the ambitions of presidents who claim to be the only authentic voice of the people?

The Benefits of the Current System

The current system teaches us that the character of a majority is more important than its size alone. Americans ought to care about whether the winner's support is spread across a broad geographic area and a wide spectrum of interests. That is what enables presidents to govern more effectively—and what encourages them to govern more justly than they would if their majority were gathered from, say, an aggregation of heavy population centers. By ensuring that the winner's majority reflects the diversity of our uniquely federated republic, the current system also assures his opposition that it will not have to fear for its life, liberty, or property. Direct election can provide no such assurance and may, in fact, guarantee just the opposite.

Appendices

Appendix A

The Amendments to the U.S. Constitution

Amendment I: Freedom of Religion, Speech, Press, Petition, and
                   Assembly (ratified 1791)
Amendment II: Right to Bear Arms (ratified 1791)
Amendment III: Quartering of Soldiers (ratified 1791)
Amendment IV: Freedom from Unfair Search and Seizures
                   (ratified 1791)
Amendment V: Right to Due Process (ratified 1791)
Amendment VI: Rights of the Accused (ratified 1791)
Amendment VII: Right to Trial by Jury (ratified 1791)
Amendment VIII: Freedom from Cruel and Unusual Punishment
                   (ratified 1791)
Amendment IX: Construction of the Constitution (ratified 1791)
Amendment X: Powers of the States and People (ratified 1791)
Amendment XI: Judicial Limits (ratified 1795)
Amendment XII: Presidential Election Process (ratified 1804)
Amendment XIII: Abolishing Slavery (ratified 1865)
Amendment XIV: Equal Protection, Due Process, Citizenship for All
                   (ratified 1868)

The Amendments to the U.S. Constitution

Amendment XV: Race and the Right to Vote (ratified 1870)
Amendment XVI: Allowing Federal Income Tax (ratified 1913)
Amendment XVII: Establishing Election to the U.S. Senate
(ratified 1913)
Amendment XVIII: Prohibition (ratified 1919)
Amendment XIX: Granting Women the Right to Vote (ratified 1920)
Amendment XX: Establishing Term Commencement for Congress
and the President (ratified 1933)
Amendment XXI: Repeal of Prohibition (ratified 1933)
Amendment XXII: Establishing Term Limits for U.S. President
(ratified 1951)
Amendment XXIII: Allowing Washington, D.C., Representation in the
Electoral College (ratified 1961)
Amendment XXIV: Prohibition of the Poll Tax (ratified 1964)
Amendment XXV: Presidential Disability and Succession
(ratified 1967)
Amendment XXVI: Lowering the Voting Age (ratified 1971)
Amendment XXVII: Limiting Congressional Pay Increases
(ratified 1992)

Appendix B

Court Cases Relevant to the Twelfth Amendment

McPherson v. Blacker, 1892
The Court held that state legislatures have the authority to choose the manner of appointment of electors.

Ray v. Blair, 1952
The U.S. Supreme Court ruled that the Twelfth Amendment does not prohibit political parties from requiring that the electors must vote for their parties' candidate. This paves the way for state parties to request guarantees from potential electors that they would only cast their electoral vote for their parties' nominee.

Buckley v. Valeo, 1976
The U.S. Supreme Court upheld the Federal Election Campaign Act limits on campaign contributions and ruled that spending money to influence elections is a form of free speech and is constitutionally protected.

Jones et al. vs. Governor George W. Bush et al., 2000
Petitioners in the case argued that Dick Cheney was ineligible to receive Texas's electors under the Constitution and the Twelfth Amendment's prohibition of both the presidential and vice presidential candidates being from the same state.

Bush v. Gore, 2000
George W. Bush challenged the Florida state supreme court ruling that ordered additional manual recounts of certain counties in the 2000 presidential election.

For Further Research

Books

George Anastaplo, *The Amendments to the Constitution: A Commentary*. Baltimore: Johns Hopkins University Press, 1995.

Robert W. Bennett, *Taming the Electoral College*. Stanford, CA: Stanford University Press, 2006.

Richard B. Bernstein with Jerome Agel, *Amending America*. New York: Times Books, 1993.

Steven J. Brams, *The Presidential Election Game*. Wellesley, MA: A.K. Peters, 2008.

Gary L. Gregg II, ed., *Securing Democracy: Why We Have an Electoral College*. Wilmington, DE: ISI Books, 2001.

Richard Johnston, Michael G. Hagen, and Kathleen Hall Jamieson, *The 2000 Presidential Election and the Foundations of Party Politics*. New York: Cambridge University Press, 2004.

Tadahisa Kuroda, *The Origins of the Twelfth Amendment*. Westport, CT: Greenwood Press, 1994.

Edward J. Larson, *A Magnificent Catastrophe: The Tumultuous Election of 1800, America's First Presidential Campaign*. New York: Free Press, 2007.

Nelson W. Polsby and Aaron Wildavsky, *Presidential Elections: Contemporary Strategies of American Electoral Politics*. New York: Free Press, 1991.

Periodicals

Paul R. Abramson et al., "Third Party and Independent Candidates in American Politics: Wallace, Anderson, and Perot." *Political Science Quarterly*, vol. 110, no. 3, Autumn 1995.

Carl Bialik, "Bad Math = Mad Politics," The Numbers Guy, *Wall Street Journal*, April 25, 2008.

David S. Broder, "A Dubious Electoral Idea," *Washington Post*, April 5, 2007.

———, "An End Run Around the Constitution," *Washington Post*, March 26, 2006.

Jonathan Chait, "Electoral College? Try Electoral Relic; There Are NO Good Arguments for Hanging on to This Anachronism," *Los Angeles Times*, October 15, 2006.

———, "Electoral College Dropouts," *Los Angeles Times*, April 9, 2006.

Dewey M. Clayton, "The Electoral College: An Idea Whose Time Has Come and Gone," *Black Scholar*, vol. 37, no. 3, Fall 2007.

E.J. Dionne Jr., "Bypassing the Electoral College," *Washington Post*, April 2, 2007.

Robert G. Dixon Jr., "Electoral College Procedure," *Western Political Quarterly*, vol. 3, no. 2, June 1950.

Randy Dotinga, "A Backdoor Plan to Thwart the Electoral College," *Christian Science Monitor*, June 16, 2006.

Bob Graham, "Forget the States—Let the Regions Pick the Candidates," *New York Times*, August 8, 2007.

Patrick Healy, "President? Or Kingmaker?" *New York Times*, June 24, 2007.

Al Kamen, "Flunking Electoral College," The Federal Page/In the Loop, *Washington Post*, November 1, 2000.

Sanford Levinson, "Our Broken Constitution," *Los Angeles Times*, October 16, 2006.

David Lublin, "Popular Vote? Not Yet; Problems with a Plan to Kill the Electoral College," *Washington Post*, July 16, 2007.

New York Times, "Abolish the Electoral College," Making Votes Count, August 29, 2004.

———, "The Case for the Electoral College," December 19, 2000.

———, "Drop Out of the College," March 14, 2006.

Washington Post, "How the Electoral College Works," November 6, 2000.

Internet Sources

William C. Kimberling, "The Electoral College," *FEC Office of Election Administration.* www.fec.gov.

———, "Origins and History of the Electoral College," *Truth Media.* www.truthinmedia.org.

William G. Ross, "'Faithless Electors': The Wild Card," *Jurist: Legal Intelligence.* http://jurist.law.pitt.edu.

Web Sites

FairVote, www.fairvote.org. This is the Web site of an organization that tries to implement change in the way elections and campaigns are run.

Federal Election Commission, www.fec.gov. The FEC regulates the funding of federal elections and campaigns. It helps ensure that all federal candidates comply with the federal campaign finance law.

National Popular Vote, www.nationalpopularvote.com. National Popular Vote is a nonprofit corporation that has the goal of replacing the current electoral system with a system whereby the president of the United States is determined based on the results of a nationwide popular election.

Index

A

Adams, John
  election as vice president, 17, 29, 56
  election of 1796, 17, 29, 78–79, 96, 102–103
  election of 1800, 13–14, 17, 26–32, 59
  Jefferson as vice president, 17, 29, 57, 96–97
  "midnight appointments" of, 32
Adams, John Quincy
  election of 1824, 19, 95
  Senate debate over Twelfth Amendment, 44
Alston, Willis, 41
Amar, Akhil Reed, 112
Amendments to the Constitution, 132–133
Aufhauser, David, 88

B

Bell, John, 123
Berenson, William, 88
Best, Judith, 112
Blacker, McPherson v., 134
Blair, Ray v., 67–71, 73–74, 134
Breckinridge, John, 45–46, 49
Breckinridge, John C., 123
Buckley v. Valeo, 134
Burr, Aaron
  challenges Jefferson in 1804, 62–64
  declares Jefferson elected in 1804, 66
  election of 1796, 17

election of 1800, 26, 27, 29, 30, 32, 62–64, 96
  portrait, *45*
Bush, George H.W., 120, 123
Bush, George W.
  election of 2000, 20, 80–89, 105–112, 116, 119, 134
  Jones v. Bush, 80–89, 134
Bush, Jeb, 110
Bush, Jones v. See Jones v. Bush
Bush v. Gore, 111, 134
Butler, Pierce, 43, 46, 52, 53

C

Cambell, Representative, 47–48
Campaigning
  election of 1800, 28
  election of 1804, 65
Campbell, G.W., 35
Cheney, Dick
  election of 2000, 80–89, 108, 134
  Jones v. Bush, 80–89, 134
  photograph, *87*
Cheney, Lynne, 87–88
Chiles, Lawton, 110
Clay, Henry, 19
Clay, J., 34–35, 36, 38
Clinton, Bill, 100, 119–120, 123
Clinton, DeWitt, 42–43
Clinton, George, 62, 66
Clopton, John, 36–37
Cocke, William, 43
Common Cause, 115
Common Sense (Paine), 15
Constitution of the United States
  amendments, 132–133